# Grilling with a Traeger

## Cookbook with 64 Recipes for the Grill Beginner and Expert

Written by

Billy Trigg

# Table Of Contents

6

# Introductions

# Some words about...

## The Traeger grill

The Traeger grill is one of the most sold products in the market today, and for good reason. Its unique design allows you to cook a variety of food items. The surface temperature can be controlled by adding or removing wood chips around the heat source.

Even the most informed people sometimes question whether it's worth making room for a grill in their lives. But when they try it out, they find that grilling is often more convenient and yields tastier steaks than using gas or charcoal.

Traeger grills are an amazing new piece of outdoor cookware. They utilize modern technologies to generate a delicious natural hardwood-fired flavor using wood as an energy fuel source for cooking your food.

If you are a conscious grill master, then perhaps a Traeger is the perfect match for your next outdoor cook-out. When using this type of grill, cooking with propane and even charcoal fumes becomes an outdated idea.

A great outdoor cooking experience should be easy and relaxing. A Traeger grill can provide this benefit by providing many years of cooking satisfaction.

If you live in a city, but don't have the option to park your grill outside because of lack of outdoor space, or if you want an easier way to grill without charcoal grilling utensils that are messy and take longer than other methods, the Traeger is a great product for you. With this appliance on your property, you can prepare with easy a lot of delicious recipes.

You can cook from the Traeger grill using a custom temperature ranging from 350 to 550 degrees. Many people have tried this product, and they found that it was more convenient and enjoyable than other brands on the market.

## How much does it cost?

This grill is quite affordable and effective when used for a long period of time. Plus, it can last longer than other grills you might consider without rusting or breaking down. The best thing about this product is that its usually less than $500 and lasts a long time so you won't have to worry about spending more money on replacement.

Using a portable grill such as the Traeger grill makes cooking easier by giving you the necessary tools you need without having to carry bulky other equipment.

Traeger grills use gas that is clean and odorless so it does not ruin the flavor of the ingredients you are cooking on them.

The Traeger is clearly worth the purchase, as you'll notice significant benefits to using it. This is especially true if you use the grill often and are able to avoid buying expensive gas grills in between.

# Shopping Guide

Traeger smokers look and behave a little differently than gas or electric appliances.

Relying on a hopper and filled cartridges in which to load entrees, such smokers produce cylindrical tubes for their food. The device works like this: first you plug it in then adjust the temperature of your fire remotely so that the smoke is controlled from an outer housing within your smoker.

There are various kinds of grill controllers:

- **Three-position controls**: Most Traeger cookers have three heat settings: low (225 degrees Fahrenheit), medium (325 degrees Fahrenheit) and high (425 degrees Fahrenheit). The temperature settings range the unit does not use a large amount of energy. We often refer to these as LMH controls.

- **Multi-position controllers**: At the push of a button, these controls can be used to adjust the temperature. Traegers are fed in set loops that allow for little precision. In optimal settings, a multi-position controller is typically accurate within 20°F of the desired temperature. The inclusion of leds is an expected function of this device.

- **Non-PID device with one-touch**: These mechanisms allow you to change the temperature in increments of 5–10 °F, which might be perfect for some types of cooking. In fixed cycles as with most products like this, they still feed traegers and therefore can offer +/- 15–20 °F accuracy. They also have LCD screens, one-touch controls.

12

- **PID controllers**: The PID controller is the gold standard of grill controls. The temperature may be off by a few degrees, but it's still pretty damn close to accurate and controllable. Programs can also control meat cooking right down to the last degree which means less time for worries about overcooking your meat or undercooking it! This thing will do all that in conjunction with your PID controller too - Traeger has you covered every step of this process thanks to its constantly controlled fuel feed so as long as everything is running smoothly there won't even need any intervention from you at all until after dinner rolls around because they've got their shit together on both sides when it comes cookin' up some BBQ goodness.

## Materials and Durability

Don't assume just because you see a Traeger grill with stainless steel that it's well-made. You could be paying for poor quality or inexpensive parts on the inside (which are often times cheaper than their more expensive counterparts).

The most important components of your grill are the fire bowl (which sits in front and lights on top), flame deflector, drop bowl, and grates. These parts are crafted from marine stainless steel because they last for a lifetime.

A stainless steel BBQ is a great choice for families. As long as the paint doesn't blister and chip, the surface won't rust for decades of family cookouts to come.

You should also remember that a traeger grill made with high-quality materials is safer. It preserves heat, allowing you to use it more effectively and helps keep the temperature at or above freezing during cold weather.

## Understanding the size of the Hopper

Not only does having a low-capacity hopper prove frustrating because it takes away much of your cook's distance, but you also run the risk of overloading and setting off your fuel-management system.

Using a traeger grill, for the most part, you will find an item with a 40-pound hopper at the standard smoking temperatures for about 40 hours. The weight of items on your smoker is important because some cooks are able to cook in 20 hours while others may need 18 pounds of fuel.

If you live in a colder climate, your cookers will push more fuel into the smokestack and maintain heat due to it.

You can buy hopper extenders for your grill to accommodate larger amounts of food. Make sure that the one you purchase is compatible with your smoker and the supplier is healthy.

## Plan How Much Cooking Real Estate You Need

You should think about how many people you're cooking for, the size of the cuts you'll be making and whether or not you plan to cook a whole animal.

Remember, bigger doesn't always mean better. A large Traeger grill can only come with more wasted food and dirty cookers.

Cooking on Traeger smokers is different than cooking in a conventional smoker because the cooking region is no longer insulated from the ambient air inside the grill.

The primary cooking area refers to the field on the central pot. The overall cooking area takes secondary racks into account

A cooker that has a limited cooking area can be an excellent option for you. This includes both a primary 450 square inch rack and a secondary 125 square inch rack, meaning that over 575 square centimeters of total effective cooking space is available

The bottom line is: make an inventory of what you need and don't assume it's cheaper.

## Common Features and Capabilities

The Traeger grill features an extensive list of cooking options. Some of the features you should consider as potential perks include:

- **Wi-Fi**: using a Wi-Fi enabled grill can make cooking so much more convenient. Grills like the Green Mountain Wireless Charcoal Barbecue are just as convenient because you use their free software to monitor and control your grill from remote locations while enjoying your meal.

- **Meat samples**: some grills with a controllable output feature can accept meat samples to be plugged directly. When the meat is done, you'll find readings updated and communicated on the cooker's computer screen automatically.

- **Grilling options**: Traeger cookers have been criticized in the past for their lack of cooking capabilities. With some models, both grilling and baking are possible by removing part of the diffuser plate or adding a special cooking area to it.

- **Add-ons**: supplement companies offer a wide range of products. Before you buy, check to see if the product includes standard features or add-ons that are extra. Some supplements have components that can be purchased separately from their manufacturers while others come with the cooker purchase.

## Length of Your Warranty

If your grill breaks down and you're not sure how to fix it, make sure you know what the warranty covers, what's void so that you don't accidentally void it, and where to get in touch with a repair technician for any part replacements.

Warranties vary for different brands of products, so it's best to ask a few questions beforehand.

## Traeger Consumption

Meat can become dried out on the outside and raw on the inside because of a too big grill.
If your grill is too large, it loses heat more quickly than cooking fires should produce. It needs to use many coals to maintain high temperatures, but this results in charcoal flavor that is hard to remove.

There are several considerations that go into the background of your chosen style of smoker. Thick walls can also be an issue for certain types of cookers because it takes a lot more fuel to reach the desired temperature in a thick-walled cooker than those with thin walls.

Find out how many traegers an hour smokers burn at different smoking temperatures. A smoker can operate continuously without harming the food with a maximum of ½ pound averaged each hour, even if it smokes at temperatures up to 1500 degrees.

## Be Cautious of Gimmicks

Traeger smokers have a lot of gimmicks and practical inventions. There is a thin distinction between the two of them, but companies want to stand out above the rest because of increasing competition among manufacturers.

Rejecting all the features on a device is not always the best approach when evaluating it in terms of its usefulness to you.

When you're trying to decide which grill is right for your particular needs, it's important to think about the features offered by each model. If a specific feature that you want isn't available in anticipation of price or convenience then that option might be out of reach.

## Customer Service

If you purchase a product or service from an established company, their customer care team is likely much larger. This means that if you require assistance the company will also be around for a while.

A smaller business may provide more consistent support, while a bigger one might not be quite so intimate.

It can be challenging to figure out whether or not a company's customer service matches its appearance.

All Traegers give you outstanding results. But, you can save a lot of money and make your meals healthier by always prefering those with high-quality materials from the start.

A reliable cooker can save you thousands in the long run, but some are unreliable and give only a one-year warranty.

With so many products being introduced these days, it can be tough to figure out which one is better and less of a risk. If you buy an expensive product without using it, that money is soon going to be wasted on replacing the unit or fixing the defect.

Please make sure to look up any information before purchasing a stove. Ask certain questions, such as what kind of gas is used and which cooktops are available. Once you know how your stove works from the top down, it's time to start cooking!

If you are planning to buy a Traeger smoker, it is very important to remember that the price range will vary significantly. This means that before you actually go shop for your top choice of brand, be sure that you've done your research on several different recommended brands.

Most people choose a traeger-style smoker because it is convenient and versatile.

You offer:

**Free from worries** - you can set the temperature of your Traeger, and just be assured that it will cook food perfectly.

**Great for the outdoors** - some traeger smokers require you to dial up to five degrees at temperature and regulate the temperature extremely well.

Cooking on a Traeger smoker can provide some other unique benefits too :

**Ultrapowerful fuel** - Traeger smokers with a super-powerful convection fan are close to your home oven, but you waste much less on traeger than on oil.

**Less energy washing** - Another potential source of frustration is the need to clean a fire pit or stove often. A traeger grill eliminates this time-consuming task with its 60-hour cooking cycle per cook, which means that it's uncommon (think about one use for each hour).

A grill is a cooking system where food rests on bars that are heated by fuel, such as wood or coal.

Before shopping for a grill, it's important to keep in mind the type of bar that you can put under your grill or stovetop.

Roundwood fire pits offer the most generous amount of product since they allow the fat of the meat to drip over from little spills on the embers. This smoke then starts to turn into tasty flavors that increase its overall value.

Most grills don't use a V-bar, seeing as people prefer to cook with fat on the grate anyways. These types of grills may have more difficulties being able to handle the food properly. This style has best been adapted for commercial cooking in restaurants or hotel rooms during meal service since it allows easier clean up and reheating over time.

In Europe, the square bar is so rare it's almost impossible to find.

Aside from configuration differences, grills are classified as fixed (standard), semi-fixed, and portable.

If you have a large garden, you may be interested in installing a grill. Grills are available in different sizes; one of the best options is one that is good for up to six people. These grills can take more time and effort to install, but they are great for country houses where there is plenty of space to accommodate them.

The semi-fixed grills have prefabricated structures that are something to place outside in a reserved space. They usually also have drawers for the ashes, so they're not scattered all over your garden when you discard them.

## BBQ : The Barbecue

The origin of the barbeque dates back several thousand years, to ancient Mesopotamia. This invention was pivotal in allowing people to make fire with controlled air flow and food still within the sealed lid served as a safe place for cooking.

The barbecue was not invented until 1950, when a man named George Steven heard about somebody else's party going wrong due to fires that ruined food.

There is nothing like cooking over an open flame. The techniques are simple and the food that comes out tasting amazing.

# Fundamentals

## Choosing Smoker

The first and most important step is to choose a smoker. There are many types of smokers available, so you can decide on how much you want to spend and which smoking method suits your preferences best: charcoal, gas, or electric.

First, future owners should use the internet to learn everything they need to know about each type of smoker before buying

A good choice for beginner cooks who want to cook meat using the smoker is one that doesn't require constant attention but has a problem of lack of flavor. On the other hand, the simplest and easiest electric smoker does not require monitoring temperature but food won't be very flavorful.

## Choosing Fuel

Smoking meat with wood chips makes the meats flavorful and gives them a distinctive flavor. Different types of wood chips have different degrees of strength; choose the type that will enhance your meat based on its thickness and taste.

## Type of Smoking Method

Smoking meat is a matter of preference. Whether you prefer to dry-season or wet-season your meat, smoke it over direct heat or indirect heat, the core difference between cold smoking and hot smoking is really just that one puts pans on their drip trays for cold smoking and barbecue grill/pan combo (or both) for hot smoking.

## Soaking Chips of Wood

Making your wood chips last longer doesn't happen by accident. The reason is that dried wood burns quickly, so adding more fuel to the smoker means less smoke penetration and dry meat at the end of the process.There is no need to soak your wood chips in water for 4 hours for them to rehydrate before smoking. Simply place aluminum foil over the bag of wood chips and poke holes in the top with a toothpick or fork.

## Set Smoker

There are many ways to start smoking, but this is the way for wood or charcoal smokers. First light up half of the charcoals then add ones they have gone down in flame and remain lit.Light your grill and wait for the coals to get heated. Remove the charcoal from one side of the grate and place your meat over that unlit part.This is done to make sure that meat is indirectly smoked over low heat. The amount of charcoal used in the smoker needs to be increased, but you should only soak wood chips if needed too.

When using your gas or electric smoker, follow manufacturer guidelines on the instructions to set up and then fill with soaked wood chips in the smoker's chip holder. To ensure that you are cooking your meat at the perfect temperature, either install an integrated thermometer or purchase one of your own.

## Selecting Meat for Smoking

This can be a decision you make as it all depends on what kind of meat should taste good with the smoky flavor:

- **Beef** : is made from different cuts of meat and includes ribs, brisket, and corned beef.

- **Pork**: spareribs, roast, shoulder (as in the cut of meat), and ham.

- **Poultry**: chicken, turkey, and game hens.

- **Seafood** : choices include salmon, scallops and trout. Lobster is a lesser-known option that can be prepared in many different ways too.

## Getting Meat Ready

Make sure you prepare meat according to the recipe provided. Doing so will ensure smoked meat turns out delicious and moist.

Aging meat utilizes a brine solution, where you mix together ingredients and pour them into a container. You soak the meat in this liquid for 8 hours, or the time recommended by your recipe. After soaking, rinse the meat thoroughly before cooking it with heat.

Marinate meats and fish in a mixture of ingredients such as olive oil, lime juice, salt, cumin seeds, garlic powder or grilled onion. Put meat or fish in the refrigerator for at least eight hours to allow the flavors and acidity to work their magic.

Rubs are commonly made with salt and spices to add a unique flavor. They must be left on the meat for at least 2 hours or more before smoking it.

Before cooking meat from the refrigerator, make sure it is at room temperature so that you can achieve a consistent internal temperature throughout.

## Placing Meat into The Smoker

Putting the meat over direct heat into a smokehouse oven is not recommended. Set aside your smoker fuel on one side and place the food on the other while leaving open space between them to allow for proper heating.

Smoking times for meat vary according to cooking method and size. For more information, please consult recipes.

## Basting Meat

Most recipes call for brushing the meat with a thin solution, sauce or marinade. This step not only makes meat taste better, but it also helps to maintain moisture and keep food moist through the smoking process. When in doubt, read your recipe better for all details needed.

When cooking meat in a smoker, remove the meat when it reaches a specific temperature. Generally, poultry should be removed from the smoker after reaching 165 degrees Fahrenheit; ground meats or hams should reach 160 degrees Fahrenheit; and chops and steaks are done at 145 degrees Fahrenheit.

# Maintenance

## Look at Manufacturer's Instructions

Traeger grills are incredibly convenient. The traeger smokers they produce come with safety information and preventative measures in place to keep their owners safe. Each model's owner's manual has official data on safety, fire-safe cooking, and maintenance procedures.

If you are a new grill owner, the most important safety step is to follow manufacturer's instructions for firing up your grill. You will need to burn off any all-important oils and bits of packaging that remain on an accessible cooking surface.

Keep your charcoal grill outside and avoid smoky, bad-tasting indoor cooking. And do not barbecue indoors in enclosed porches or tents as those areas are also unsafe.

To stay safe and avoid safety hazards, keep the following safety tips in mind at all times.

## Safety

Keep fire extinguishers within reach in both your kitchen and outdoor grill areas.

Don't try to move a hot grill, it can explode.

Follow these common safety practices when using a propane grill. This will help ensure that the fire pot and its auger are cleared regularly, preventing the accumulation of goo visible as black sludge at the opening of your fire pot.

Keep kids, pets, and flammable liquids away from the grill at all times during cooking -cast-iron grills can start fires if not watched closely.

Try not to eat while cooking with strange wood, especially traegers that were not specifically designed for cooking. Non-food safe grills can be comprised of scrap wood, which is often treated with toxic chemicals and undesirable finishes that you wouldn't want to consume.

Because grill manufacturers don't want you to leave their cookers on all day, they mention in the owner's manual that it's important not to overdo it and avoid burning food. They also warn that only permitting your children access while the fires are still burning is dangerous.

Do not use your traeger grill in wet weather or keep it uncovered because the moist air will ruin it, and you are also likely to catch a dangerous shock when touching any electrical components.

Unplug your BBQ when not in use, and be mindful of the risks associated with electrical cords. Remember that you won't work your BBQ if it loses power.

There's no need to always be a slave to flipping wood and cooking over an open fire. These days, you can use the Traeger grill as your go-to method of grilling anything in minutes with convenience that tastes so much better than charcoal and stick smokers without sacrificing safety by switching up their process. The traeger grill has a small fire that burns inside of it and heats up automatically.

Make sure that you always use your manufacturer's start-up and shutdown procedures.

To maintain fuel efficiency, it is important to clean the fire grate and auger during normal use.

If your grill's heat is struggling, it could be because of the outside temperature. A number of different factors can cause this such as windy conditions or cold temperatures, but one thing you may need to do is compensate for the cooker being off-balance in a specific direction.

If you find that your cooking times are longer than normal, it is worth evaluating whether or not you are being plagued by prying eyes. In most cases, a traeger grill's thermostat can combat this issue better than other types of smokers.

A grill, sadly, is not a phoenix; it needs to be cleaned often. This includes before the procedure or at least 12 hours after any ignition

If you use a traeger-style barbecue grill, make sure you have an electrical outlet nearby. A blown fuse or power interruption can prevent food from cooking properly and ruining your meal supplies.

Keep the grill well-lubricated to prevent sticking when cooking on it. Clean up excess ash from the fire pot and cook chamber as required.

Vacuum the areas in and around the hopper, especially after use.

Always scrub your grill grate after each use to keep the porcelain finish protected.

Do not use sprays or liquid cleaners on your traeger to clean it.

Cover the grill when not in use so it doesn't get bleached or moistened, and to avoid any insects being attracted to it.

If you have trouble turning on your grill, make sure the fire pot is intact. If not, it may be due to poor maintenance or corrosion over time. You can replace the fire pot with any metal alloy of your preference; for example stainless-steel.

# The World of Accessories

## Tools and Gadgets

Spending time on the weekends perfecting your grilling skills can be enjoyable, but not when you have to rely on unfamiliar tools and gadgets. Below is a list of my favorite tools and gadgets which you're going to wish you had as soon as cooking with them begins.

### Must-Haves

**THERMOMETER**: Everyone has a good old-fashioned meat thermometer in the kitchen. However, I have noticed a significant price drop recently in quality, instant-read digital thermometers that are better than the analog ones. Ten dollars on Amazon will get you a reliable probe with an easy way to read the temperature so you can cook confidently.

**MOP**: The professional barbecue chef uses a full-size cotton mop to apply basting sauces over their heavy hams or beef briskets. For smaller applications, the most common model has been scaled down into an even smaller version which can still soak in tons of gravy at once.

**SPRAY BOTTLE**: Look in your grocery store or at Wal-Mart for food-safe, empty bottles to fill with sauces. They should have a narrow opening and no clumps or chunky spices that will block the needle. They should also be washable so you can reuse them over and over again.

**INJECTOR**: These tools allow you to inject marinade into your meat from the inside out, mimicking commercial grade without breaking the bank.

**FIRE EXTINGUISHER**: I think it's reasonable to have two fire extinguishers: one for the kitchen and one near the patio. If you don't, I would suggest investing in a small carbon monoxide (CO) detector as a first step towards being able to quickly identify CO problems too.

**GLOVES**: Grilling meat can be tough, but gloves make it easier even if you don't want to handle the raw meat by hand.

**HEAVY-DUTY ALUMINUM FOIL**: Find aluminum foil at large grocery stores and use it to cover whole roasts, lining drip pans

## More Toys

**NONSTICK GRILL MATS**: These heat-resistant mesh mats help make rearranging smoker cleanup a breeze. These mats allow you to use them with pretty much any type and size of smoker, but they really excel when used on smokers that have built-in small openings in the smoke chamber instead of large doors or top vents.

**PERFORATED PIZZA SCREEN**: These plastic pizza screens are great for grilling on a barbecue in place of grill mats. They're inexpensive, reusable, dishwasher safe, and easy to store.

**GRILL BRUSH/SCRAPER**: You should keep wire-bristled brushes away from the grill. Though they make cleaning a good job, bristles can become loose and fall into your food. Also, I would never place my hand over a BBQ grate that has been coated with porcelain in order to clean it off; these are delicate surfaces.

**RIB RACK**: Some grates have a smaller usable size than others. A standard dome lid can be difficult to use, so if you want to maximize your space on the grill, consider using a rib rack.

**BEAR CLAWS**: There are many manufacturers who make different variations of fork attachments (specifically designed for Boston butts and not necessary). The most important features to look for include being heat resistant, made out of an appropriate material (either hard plastic, heat-resistant claws, or stainless steel tines), and affordable.

# How to Clean Your Grill

## Cleaning and Sanitization

Traeger grills are easy to clean because they don't get that grimy quickly. Traditional grills require a lot of cleaning and can be frustrating to use especially if you have busy schedules.

**1.** Open the lid of your grill, and then use a dry cloth to wipe down the grates. After this, you can choose between a peeler for scrubbing or a brush for cleaning the back wall. Emptying all dirt into a drip tray is an effective way to keep your grill clean.

**2.** While you are scrubbing the inside of the smoke exhaust, make sure to open your grease bucket.

**3.** You can make this easier on yourself by taking out the drip pan and replacing it with a fresh aluminum foil.

**4.** Siphon the ash from below the fire using a vacuum on the inside of your firepot.

**5.** If you're trying to clean the exterior of an outdoor grill without taking it apart, you can use a cleaner with water on a long-handled spray bottle. Spray it over the important parts of the grill while being careful not to wet the electronic controls, then wait one minute before wiping down everything with a damp cloth.

**More Tips:**

- Another important step when cleaning a grill is to make sure it's completely cooled off first before you take the opportunity to scrub and clean anything up.

- Vacuum the insides of the Traeger Hopper to get any ash or dust.

- Folded paper towel rolls are a great way to keep your temperature probes clean, especially since you can buy them inexpensively at any gas station or hardware store.

- Clean and sanitize all surfaces as needed. Be careful when drawing out the grate since you may damage or scrape the temperature probe.

- Always replace the aluminum foil every time you grill meat. This will ensure that the smoke flavours remain pure and that no particulates from previous grilling sessions get stuck to what is currently being prepared.

- Use grease liners or aluminum foil in the grease bucket to make cleanup easier. Put your used oil down a trashcan since this will clog your pipes.

## Cooking Temperatures, Times, and Doneness

Here are some approximate cooking times for the different temperature settings so you can do a better recipe.

### Fish and Seafood

- **White fish and Salmon** : can be grilled at 400-450 degrees Fahrenheit for 5-8 minutes on each side or until flaky.

- **Steamed lobster** : should be cooked at 200–225 degrees Fahrenheit for 15 minutes per pound of lobster.

- **Scallops** : cook at 190 degrees Fahrenheit from 1 to 1.5 hours.

- **Shrimps** : cook at 400–450 degrees Fahrenheit for 4–5 minutes per side.

## Pork

- **Pork ribs** : can be smoked at a temperature of 275 degrees Fahrenheit for three to six hours

- **Pork loin** : cooks at 410 degrees Fahrenheit exactly until the internal temperature reaches 150 – 180 degrees Fahrenheit

- **Pulled pork butt** : should be cooked at a temperature of 230–255 degrees Fahrenheit, until it reaches 210 degrees Fahrenheit.

- **Bacon and sausages** : should be cooked at 430 degrees Fahrenheit for 6-7 minutes on each side or until cooked.

## Beef

- **Beef short ribs** : cooks at 230–255 degrees Fahrenheit for 4–6 hours until the meat can be easily pulled off of the bone.

- **Beef brisket** : cooks at 250 degrees Fahrenheit for 4 hours then covered with foil to cook for another 4 hours or more.

- **Medium rare beef tenderloin** : should be cooked at 230–255 degrees Fahrenheit for 3 hours but Beef jerky needs a low heat setting at least for 4–5 hours.

## Poultry

- **Whole chicken** : should be cooked at 405 degrees Fahrenheit until internal temp reaches 170 degrees Fahrenheit.

- **Chicken breast** : needs 405 degrees Fahrenheit and 14-15 minutes on each side.

- **Pheasant** : should be cooked at 200 degrees Fahrenheit for 2–3 hours until internal temp reaches 165 degrees Fahrenheit.
- **Smoked turkey** : should be cooked at 185–220 degrees Fahrenheit for 10–12 hours or until the internal temp is 170 degrees Fahrenheit.

# Recipes

# Chicken

## 1.1 - Smoked Chicken Thighs

Preparation time: 20 minutes
Cooking time: 24 minutes
Servings: **6**

*Ingredients:*

- 6 chicken thighs
- ½ cup commercial BBQ sauce of your choice 1 ½ tbsp. poultry spice 4 tbsp. butter

*Directions:*

1. Place all ingredients in a bowl except for the butter. Massage the chicken to make sure that the chicken is coated with the marinade.
2. Place in the fridge to marinate for 4 hours.
3. Fire the Traeger Grill to 350°F. Use hickory traegers. Close the lid and preheat for 15 minutes.
4. When ready to cook, place the chicken on the grill grate and cook for 12 minutes on each side.
5. Before serving the chicken, brush with butter on top.

*Nutritional Values (Per Serving):*

**Calories: 504**

Carbs: 2.7g
Fat: 39.9g
Protein: 32.4g
Sugar: 0.9g

## 1.2 - Spiced Lemon Chicken

Preparation time: 30 minutes
Cooking time: 0 minutes
Servings: **1**

*Ingredients:*

- 1 whole chicken
- 4 cloves minced garlic
- Zest 2 fresh lemons
- 1 tbsp. olive oil
- 1 tbsp. smoked paprika
- 1 ½ tsp. salt
- ½ tsp. black pepper
- ½ tsp. dried oregano
- 1 tbsp. ground cumin

*Directions:*

1. Preheat the grill by pushing the temperature to 375°F
2. Now take the chicken and spatchcock it by cutting it on both the sides right from the backbone to the tail via the neck
3. Lay it flat and push it down on the breastbone. This would break the ribs
4. Take all the leftover ingredients in a bowl except ½ tsp. of salt and crush them to make a smooth rub
5. Spread this rub evenly over the chicken making sure that it seeps right under the skin
6. Now place the chicken on the grill grates and let it cook for an hour until the internal temperature reads 165°F
7. Let it rest for 10 minutes

8. Serve and enjoy

**Calories: 490**

Carbs: 39 g
Cholesterol: 19 mg
Protein: 29 g
Sodium: 15 mg

## 1.3 - Whole Smoked Chicken

Preparation time: 30 minutes
Cooking time: 3 hours
Servings: **6**

*Ingredients:*

- ½ cup salt
- 1 cup brown sugar:
- 1 whole chicken (3 ½ pounds)
- 1 tsp. minced garlic
- 1 lemon, halved
- 1 medium onion, quartered
- 3 whole cloves
- 5 sprigs of thyme

*Directions:*

1. Dissolve the salt and sugar in 4 liters of water. Once dissolved, place the chicken in the brine and let marinate for 24 hours.
2. When ready to cook, fire the Traeger Grill up to 250°F and allow to preheat for 15 minutes with the lid closed. Use any traeger desired but we recommend using the maple traeger.
3. While the grill is preheating, remove the chicken from the brine and pat dry using paper towel.
4. Rub the minced garlic all over the chicken. Stuff the cavity of the chicken with the remaining ingredients.
5. Tie the legs together with a natural string.

6. Place the stuffed chicken directly on the grill grate and smoke for 3 hours until the internal temperature of the chicken is 160°F particularly in the breast part.
7. Take the chicken out and grill.

*Nutritional Values (Per Serving):*

**Calories: 251**

Carbs: 19g
Fat: 4.3g
Protein: 32.6g
Sugar: 17.3g

## 1.4 - Grilled Asian Chicken Burgers

Preparation time: 5 minutes
Cooking time: 50 minutes
Servings: **4-6**

*Ingredients:*

- Pound chicken, ground
- 1 cup panko breadcrumbs
- 1 cup parmesan cheese
- 1 small jalapeno, diced
- 2 whole scallions, minced
- 2 garlic clove
- ¼ cup minced cilantro leaves
- 2 tbsp. mayonnaise
- 2 tbsp. chili sauce
- 1 tbsp. soy sauce
- 1 tbsp. ginger, minced
- 2 tsp. lemon juice
- 2 tsp. lemon zest
- 1 tsp. salt
- 1 tsp. ground black pepper
- 8 hamburger buns
- 1 tomato, sliced
- Arugula, fresh
- 1 red onion sliced

*Directions:*

1. Align a rimmed baking sheet with aluminum foil then spray with nonstick cooking spray.

2. In a large bowl, combine the chicken, jalapeno, scallion, garlic, cilantro, panko, Parmesan, chili sauce, soy sauce ginger, mayonnaise, lemon juice and zest, and salt and pepper.
3. Work the mixture with your fingers until the ingredients are well combined. If the mixture looks too wet to form patties and add additional more panko.
4. Wash your hands under cold running water, form the meat into 8 patties, each about an inch larger than the buns and about ¾" thick.
5. Use your thumbs or a tbsp., make a wide, shallow depression in the top of each
6. Put them on the prepared baking sheet. Spray the tops with nonstick cooking spray. If not cooking right away, cover with plastic wrap and refrigerate.
7. Set the traeger grill to 350°F then preheat for 15 minutes, lid closed.
8. Order the burgers, depression-side down, on the grill grate. Remove and discard the foil on the baking sheet so you'll have an uncontaminated surface to transfer the slider when cooked.
9. Grill the burgers for about 25 to 30 minutes, turning once, or until they release easily from the grill grate when a clean metal spatula is slipped under them. The internal temperature when read on an instant-read meat thermometer should be 160°F.
10. Spread mayonnaise and arrange a tomato slice, if desired, and a few arugula leaves on one-half of each bun. Top with a grilled burger and red onions, if using, then replace the top half of the bun. Serve immediately. Enjoy!

*Nutritional Values (Per Serving):*

**Calories: 329**

Carbs: 10g
Fat: 23g
Protein: 21g

## 1.5 - Whole Orange Chicken

Preparation time: 15 minutes + marinate time
Cooking time: 45 minutes
Servings: **4**

*Ingredients:*

- 1 whole chicken, 3–4 pounds' backbone removed
- 2 oranges
- ¼ cup oil
- 2 tsp. Dijon mustard
- 1 orange, zest
- 2 tbsp. rosemary leaves, chopped
- 2 tsp. salt

*Directions:*

1. Clean and pat your chicken dry
2. Take a bowl and mix in orange juice, oil, orange zest, salt, rosemary leaves, Dijon mustard and mix well
3. Marinade chicken for 2 hours or overnight
4. Pre-heat your grill to 350°F
5. Transfer your chicken to the smoker and smoke for 30 minutes' skin down. Flip and smoke until the internal temperature reaches 175°F in the thigh and 165°F in the breast
6. Rest for 10 minutes and carve
7. Enjoy!

*Nutritional Values (Per Serving):*

## Calories: 290

Carbs: 20g
Fats: 15g
Fiber: 1g

Preparation time: 30 minutes
Cooking time: 3 Hours
Servings: **1**

*Ingredients:*

- 4 pounds of chicken with the giblets thoroughly removed and patted dry
- 1 ½ lemon
- 1 tbsp. honey
- 4 tbsp. unsalted butter
- 4 tbsp. chicken seasoning

*Directions:*

1. Fire up your smoker and set the temperature to 225°F
2. Take a small saucepan and melt the butter along with honey over a low flame
3. Now squeeze ½ lemon in this mixture and then move it from the heat source
4. Take the chicken and smoke by keeping the skin side down. Do so until the chicken turns light brown and the skin starts to release from the grate.
5. Turn the chicken over and apply the honey butter mixture to it
6. Continue to smoke it making sure to taste it every 45 minutes until the thickest core reaches a temperature of 160°F
7. Now remove the chicken from the grill and let it rest for 5 minutes
8. Serve with the leftover sliced lemon and enjoy.

## Nutritional Values (Per Serving):

**Calories: 380**

Carbs: 29 g
Cholesterol: 19 mg
Protein: 19 g
Sodium: 25 mg

Preparation time: 10 minutes
Cooking time: 10 minutes
Servings: **10**

*Ingredients:*

- 2 lb. chicken breast
- 1 onion, sliced
- 1 red bell pepper, seeded and sliced
- 1 orange-red bell pepper, seeded and sliced
- 1 tbsp. salt
- ½ tbsp. onion powder
- ½ tbsp. granulated garlic
- 2 tbsp. Spiceologist Chile Margarita Seasoning
- 2 tbsp. oil

*Directions:*

1. Preheat the Traeger to 450°F and line a baking sheet with parchment paper.
2. In a mixing bowl, combine seasonings and oil then toss with the peppers and chicken.
3. Place the baking sheet in the Traeger and let heat for 10 minutes with the lid closed.
4. Open the lid and place the veggies and the chicken in a single layer. Close the lid and cook for 10 minutes or until the chicken is no longer pink.
5. Serve with warm tortillas and top with your favorite toppings.

*Nutritional Values (Per Serving):*

## Calories: 211

Fat: 6g
Fiber: 1g
Protein: 29g
Sodium: 360mg

## 1.8 - Lemon Rosemary and Beer Marinated Chicken

Preparation time: 20 minutes
Cooking time: 35 minutes
Servings: **6**

*Ingredients:*

- 1 whole chicken
- 1 lemon, zested and juiced
- 1 tsp. salt
- 1 tsp. ground black pepper
- 1 tsp. rosemary, chopped
- 12-ounce beer, apple-flavored

*Directions:*

1. Place all ingredients in a bowl and allow the chicken to marinate for at least 12 hours in the fridge.
2. When ready to cook, fire the Traeger Grill to 350°F. Use preferred traegers. Close the grill lid and preheat for 15 minutes.
3. Place the chicken on the grill grate and cook for 55 minutes.
4. Cook until the internal temperature reads 165°F.
5. Take the chicken out and allow to rest before carving.

## Nutritional Values (Per Serving):

**Calories: 288**

Carbs: 4.4g
Fat: 13.1g
Protein: 36.1g
Sugar: 0.7g

## 1.9 - Lemon Chicken Breasts

Preparation time: 20 minutes
Cooking time: 40 minutes
Servings: **6**

*Ingredients:*

- 1 clove of garlic, minced
- 2 tsp. honey
- 2 tsp. salt
- 1 tsp. black pepper, ground
- 2 sprigs fresh thyme leaves
- 1 lemon, zested and juiced
- ½ cup olive oil
- 6 boneless chicken breasts

*Directions:*

1.  Make the marinade by combining the garlic, honey, salt, pepper, thyme, lemon zest, and juice in a bowl. Whisk until well-combined.
2.  Place the chicken into the marinade and mix with hands to coat the meat with the marinade. Refrigerate for 4 hours.
3.  When ready to grill, fire the Traeger Grill to 400°F. Close the lid and preheat for 10 minutes.
4.  Drain the chicken and discard the marinade.
5.  Arrange the chicken breasts directly on to the grill grate and cook for 40 minutes or until the internal temperature of the thickest part of the chicken reaches 165°F.
6.  Drizzle with more lemon juice before serving.

**Calories: 669**

Carbs: 3g
Fat: 44.9g
Protein: 60.6g
Sugar: 2.1g

# Beef

## 2.1 - BBQ Meatloaf

Preparation time: 20 minutes
Cooking time: 2½ hours
Servings: **8**

*Ingredients:*

For Meatloaf:
- 3 pounds ground beef
- 3 eggs
- ½ cup panko breadcrumbs
- 1 (10-ounce) can diced tomatoes with green chile peppers
- 1 large white onion, chopped
- 2 hot banana peppers, chopped
- 2 tbsp. seasoned salt
- 2 tsp. liquid smoke flavoring
- 2 tsp. smoked paprika
- 1 tsp. onion salt
- 1 tsp. garlic salt
- Salt and ground black pepper, as required
  For Sauce:
- ½ cup ketchup
- ¼ cup tomato-based chile sauce
- ¼ cup white Sugar:
- 2 tsp. Worcestershire sauce
- 2 tsp. hot pepper sauce
- 1 tsp. red pepper flakes, crushed
- 1 tsp. red chili pepper
- Salt and ground black pepper, as required

1. Preheat the Z Grills Traeger Grill & Smoker on smoke setting to 225°F, using charcoal.
2. Grease a loaf pan.
3. For the meatloaf: in a bowl, add all ingredients, and with your hands, mix until well combined.
4. Place the mixture into the prepared loaf pan evenly.
5. Place the pan onto the grill and cook for about 2 hours.
6. For the sauce: in a bowl, add all ingredients and beat until well combined.
7. Remove the pan from the grill and drain excess grease from the meatloaf.
8. Place sauce over meatloaf evenly and place the pan onto the grill.
9. Cook for about 30 minutes.
10. Remove the meatloaf from the grill and set aside for about 10 minutes before serving.
11. Carefully, invert the meatloaf onto a platter.
12. Cut the meatloaf into desired-sized slices and serve.

*Nutritional Values (Per Serving):*

**Calories: 423**

Carbs: 15.7 g
Cholesterol: 213 mg
Fat: 13 g
Fiber: 1.5 g
Protein: 54.9 g
Saturated Fat: 4.7 g
Sodium: 1879 mg
Sugar: 12.3 g

Preparation time: 20 minutes
Cooking time: 1 hour
Servings: **6**

*Ingredients:*

- 6 large bell peppers
- 1 pound ground beef
- 1 small onion, chopped
- 2 garlic cloves, minced
- 2 cups cooked rice
- 1 cup frozen corn, thawed
- 1 cup cooked black beans
- 2/3 cup salsa
- 2 tbsp. Cajun rub
- 1½ cups Monterey Jack cheese, grated

*Directions:*

1. Cut each bell pepper in half lengthwise through the stem.
2. Carefully, remove the seeds and ribs.
3. For stuffing: heat a large frying pan and cook the beef for about 6-7 minutes or until browned completely.
4. Add onion and garlic and cook for about 2-3 minutes.
5. Stir in remaining ingredients except for cheese and cook for about 5 minutes.
6. Remove from the heat and set aside to cool slightly.
7. Preheat the Z Grills Traeger Grill & Smoker on grill setting to 350°F.
8. Stuff each bell pepper half with stuffing mixture evenly.

9.  Arrange the peppers onto grill, stuffing side up, and cook for about 40 minutes.
10. Sprinkle each bell pepper half with cheese and cook for about 5 minutes more.
11. Remove the bell peppers from grill and serve hot.

*Nutritional Values (Per Serving):*

**Calories: 675**

Carbs: 90.7 g
Cholesterol: 93 mg
Fat: 14.8 g
Fiber: 8.7 g
Protein: 43.9 g
Saturated Fat: 7.5 g
Sodium: 1167 mg
Sugar: 9.1 g

## 2.3 - Traeger Smoked Rib-eye Steaks

Preparation time: 15 minutes
Cooking time: 35 minutes
Servings: **1**

*Ingredients:*

- 2-inch thick rib-eye steaks
- Steak rub of choice

*Directions:*

1. Preheat your traeger grill to low smoke.
2. Sprinkle the steak with your favorite steak rub and place it on the grill. Let it smoke for 25 minutes.
3. Remove the steak from the grill and set the temperature to 400°F.
4. Return the steak to the grill and sear it for 5 minutes on each side.
5. Cook until the desired temperature is achieved, 125°F-rare, 145°F-Medium, and 165°F.-Well done.
6. Wrap the steak with foil and let rest for 10 minutes before serving. Enjoy.

*Nutritional Values (Per Serving):*

**Calories: 225**

Fat: 10.4g
Fiber: 0g
Protein: 32.5g
Sodium: 63mg
Sugar: 0g

## 2.4 - Grilled Beef Steak with Peanut Oil and Herbs

Preparation time: 4 hours and 45 minutes
Cooking time: 55 minutes
Servings: **6**

*Ingredients:*

- 3 lbs. beef steak, preferably flank
- 1 tsp. sea salt
- 2 tbsp. peanut oil
- ¼ olive oil
- 2 tbsp. fresh mint leaves, finely chopped
- 2 tsp. peppercorn black
- 2 tsp. peppercorn green
- ½ tsp. cumin seeds
- 1 pinch of chili flakes

*Directions:*

1. Rub the beef steaks with coarse salt and place in a large dish.
2. Make a marinade, in a bowl, combine peanut oil, olive oil, fresh mint leave, peppercorn, cumin, and chili flakes.
3. Cover and refrigerate for 4 hours.
4. Bring the meat to room temperature 30 minutes before you put it on the grill.
5. Start your traeger grill, set the temperature on High and preheat, lid closed, for 10 to 15 minutes.
6. As a general rule, you should grill steaks on high heat (450–500°F).

7. Grill about 7–10 minutes per side at high temperatures or 15–20 minutes per side at the lower temperatures, or to your preference for doneness.
8. Remove flank steak from the grill and let cool before slicing for 10 -15 minutes.
9. Slice and serve.

*Nutritional Values (Per Serving):*

**Calories: 346.3**

Carbs: 0.21g
Fat: 15.15g
Fiber: 0.07g
Protein: 32.38g

Preparation time: 15 minutes
Cooking time: 40 minutes
Servings: **4**

*Ingredients:*

- 4 tbsp. butter, melted
- 2 tbsp. Worcestershire sauce
- 2 tbsp. Dijon mustard
- Traeger Prime rib rub

*Directions:*

1. Set your traeger grill to 225°F with the lid closed for 15 minutes.
2. In a mixing bowl, mix butter, sauce, Dijon mustard until smooth. brush the mixture on the meat then season with the rub.
3. Arrange the meat on the grill grate and cook for 30 minutes.
4. Use tongs to transfer the meat to a patter then increase the heat to high.
5. Return the meat to the grill grate to grill until your desired doneness is achieved.
6. Baste with the butter mixture again if you desire and let rest for 3 minutes before serving. Enjoy.

*Nutritional Values (Per Serving):*

**Calories: 726**

Fat: 62g
Fiber: 1g
Protein: 36g
Sodium: 97mg
Sugar: 1g

## 2.6 - Prime Rib Roast

Preparation time: 24 hours
Cooking time: 4 hours and 30 minutes
Servings: **8**

*Ingredients:*

- 1 prime rib roast, containing 5 to 7 bones Rib rub as needed

*Directions:*

1. Season rib roast with rib rub until well coated, place it in a large plastic bag, seal it and let it marinate for a minimum of 24 hours in the refrigerator.
2. When ready to cook, switch on the Traeger grill, fill the grill hopper with cherry flavored traegers, power the grill on by using the control panel, select 'smoke' on the temperature dial, or set the temperature to 225°F and let it preheat for a minimum of 15 minutes.
3. When the grill has preheated, open the lid, place rib roast on the grill grate fat-side up, change the smoking temperature to 425°F, shut the grill, and smoke for 30 minutes.
4. Then change the smoking temperature to 325°F and continue cooking for 3 to 4 hours until roast has cooked to the desired level, rare at 120°F, medium rare at 130°F, medium at 140°F, and well done at 150°F.
5. When done, transfer roast rib to a cutting board, let it rest for 15 minutes, then cut it into slices and serve.

*Nutritional Values (Per Serving):*

**Calories: 248**

Fat: 21.2 g
Protein: 28 g

Preparation time: 20 minutes
Cooking time: 6 hours
Servings: **6**

*Ingredients:*

- 4 lb. beef sirloin tip roast
- ½ cup barbecue rub
- 2 bottles amber beer
- 1 bottle barbecue sauce

*Directions:*

1. Turn your traeger grill onto the smoke setting then trim excess fat from the steak.
2. Coat the steak with barbecue rub and let it smoke on the grill for 1 hour.
3. Continue cooking and flipping the steak for the next 3 hours. Transfer the steak to a braising vessel. Add the beers.
4. Braise the beef until tender then transfer to a platter reserving 2 cups of cooking liquid.
5. Use a pair of forks to shred the beef and return it to the pan. Add the reserved liquid and barbecue sauce. Stir well and keep warm before serving.

## Nutritional Values (Per Serving):

**Calories: 829**

Fat: 46g
Fiber: 0g
Protein: 86g
Saturated Fat: 18g
Sodium: 181mg

## 2.8 - Simple Smoked Beef Brisket with Mocha Sauce

Preparation time: 15 minutes
Cooking time: 1 hour
Servings: **10**

*Ingredients:*

- 5 pounds beef brisket
- 1 ½ tbsp. garlic powder
- 1 ½ tbsp. onion powder
- 4 tbsp. salt
- 4 tbsp. pepper
- 2 ½ tbsp. olive oil
- 1 cup chopped onion
- 2 tsp. salt
- ¼ cup chopped chocolate dark
- ¼ cup sugar
- ½ cup beer
- 2 shots espresso

*Directions:*

1. Rub the beef brisket with garlic powder, onion powder, salt, and black pepper.
2. Wrap the seasoned beef brisket with a sheet of plastic wrap then store in the refrigerator overnight.
3. In the morning, remove the beef brisket from the refrigerator and thaw for about an hour.
4. Preheat the smoker to 250°F (121°C) with charcoal and hickory chips , using indirect heat. Place the beef brisket in the smoker and smoke for 8 hours.

5. Keep the temperature remain at 250°F (121°C) and add some more charcoal and hickory chips if it is necessary.
6. Meanwhile, preheat a saucepan over medium heat then pour olive oil into the saucepan.
7. Once the oil is hot, stir in chopped onion then sauté until wilted and aromatic.
8. Reduce the heat to low then add the remaining sauce ingredients to the saucepan. Mix well then bring to a simmer.
9. Remove the sauce from heat then set aside.
10. When the smoked beef brisket is ready, or the internal temperature has reached 190°F (88°C), remove from the smoker then transfer to a serving dish.
11. Drizzle the mocha sauce over the smoked beef brisket then serve.
12. Enjoy warm.

*Nutritional Values (Per Serving):*

**Calories: 210**

Carbs: 1g
Fat: 13g
Protein: 19g

# Pork

Preparation time: 24 Hours
Cooking time: 15 minutes
Servings: **6**

*Ingredients:*

---

- 3 lbs. Pork tenderloin
- 3 cup margarita mix
- 3 clove garlic, minced
- 2 large bell peppers
- 4 lbs. whole mushrooms
- ¼ cup butter, softened
- 4 tsp. lime juice
- 1 tsp. Sugar:
- 3 tbsp. minced parsley

*Directions:*

---

1. Cut pork into 1-inch cubes, place in a sealable plastic bag, pour marinade over to cover. Marinate overnight.
2. Blend together the butter, lime juice, Splenda, and parsley, set aside.
3. Thread pork cubes onto skewers, alternating with mushrooms and pepper, cut into eighths.
4. Grill over high heat, basting with butter mixture, for 10–15 minutes, turning frequently.
5. If you're using bamboo skewers, soak them in water 20–30 minutes before using.

*Nutritional Values (Per Serving):*

## Calories: 160

Carbs: 2g
Fat: 5g
Protein: 28g

## 3.2 - Pulled Hickory-Smoked Pork Butts

Preparation time: 30 to 45 minutes
Cooking time: 6 hours
Servings: **20**

*Ingredients:*

- Traeger: Hickory
- 2 (10-pound) boneless pork butts, vacuum-stuffed or fresh
- 1 cup roasted garlic-seasoned extra-virgin olive oil
- ¾ cup Pork Dry Rub, Jan's Original Dry Rub, or your preferred pork rub

*Directions:*

1. Trim the fat cap and any effectively available enormous segments of abundance fat from every pork butt as you see fit.
2. Remove the pork butts from the grill and double wrap everyone in heavy-duty aluminum foil. Take care to ensure that you keep your meat probes in the butts as you double-wrap them.
3. Return the wrapped pork butts to your 350°F traeger smoker-grill.
4. Keep cooking the foil-wrapped pork butts until the internal temperature of the pork butts arrives at 200°F to 205°F.
5. Remove the pork butts and FTC them for 3 to 4 hours before pulling and serving.
6. Force the smoked pork butts into minimal succulent shreds utilizing your preferred pulling technique. I prefer utilizing my hands while wearing heat-safe gloves.

7. On the off chance that you'd like, blend the pulled pork butts with any remaining fluids.
8. Serve the pulled pork with grill sauce on a fresh-prepared mould topped with coleslaw, or serve the pulled pork with sides like lettuce, tomato, red onion, mayo, cheese, and horseradish.

*Nutritional Values (Per Serving):*

**Calories: 267**

Fat: 18 g
Protein: 25 g

### 3.3 - Smoked Pork Cutlets with Caraway and Dill

Preparation time: 15 minutes
Cooking time: 1 hour 30 minutes
Servings: **4**

*Ingredients:*

---

- 4 pork cutlets
- 2 lemons freshly squeezed
- 2 tbs. fresh parsley finely chopped
- 1 tbsp. ground caraway
- 3 tbsp. fresh dill finely chopped
- ¼ cup olive oil
- salt and ground black pepper

*Directions:*

---

1. Place the pork cutlets in a large resealable bag along with all remaining ingredients, shake to combine well.
2. Refrigerate for at least 4 hours.
3. Remove the pork cutlets from the marinade and pat dry on a kitchen towel.
4. Start the traeger grill (recommended maple traeger) on SMOKE with the lid open until the fire is established. Set the temperature to 250°F and preheat, lid closed, for 10 to 15 minutes.
5. Arrange pork cutlets on the grill rack and smoke for about 1 and a half hours.
6. Allow cooling at room temperature before serving.

## Nutritional Values (Per Serving):

**Calories: 308**

Carbs: 2.4g
Fat: 18.5g
Fiber: 0.36g
Protein: 32g

Preparation time: 15 minutes
Cooking time: 0 minutes
Servings: **12**

*Ingredients:*

- 4 pounds' boneless center-cut pork (trimmed of excess fat and sliced into ¼ inch thick slices)
- Marinade:
- 1/3 cup soy sauce
- 1 cup pineapple juice
- 1 tbsp. rice wine vinegar
- 2 tsp. black pepper
- 1 tsp. red pepper flakes
- 5 tbsp. brown sugar:
- 1 tsp. paprika
- 1 tsp. onion powder
- 1 tsp. garlic powder
- 2 tsp. salt or to taste

*Directions:*

1. Combine and mix all the marinade ingredients in a mixing bowl.
2. Put the sliced pork in a gallon-sized zip-lock bag and pour the marinade into the bag. Massage the marinade into the pork. Seal the bag and refrigerate for 8 hours.
3. Activate the pellet grill smoker setting and leave the lip open for 5 minutes until the fire starts.
4. Close the lid and preheat your pellet grill to 180°F, using a hickory pellet.

5. Remove the pork slices from the marinade and pat them dry with a paper towel.
6. Arrange the pork slices on the grill in a single layer. Smoke the pork for about 2 ½ hours, often turning after the first 1 hour of smoking. The jerky should be dark and dry when it is done.
7. Remove the jerky from the grill and let it sit for about 1 hour to cool.
8. Serve immediately or store in airtight containers and refrigerate for future use.

*Nutritional Values (Per Serving):*

**Calories: 260**

Carbohydrate: 8.6g
Cholesterol: 80mg
Fat: 11.4g
Protein: 28.1g

## 3.5 - Braised Pork Chile Verde

Preparation time: 10 minutes
Cooking time: 40 minutes
Servings: **6**

*Ingredients:*

- 3 pounds' pork shoulder, bone removed and cut into ½ inch cubes
- 1 tbsp. all-purpose flour
- Salt and pepper to taste
- 1-pound tomatillos, husked and washed
- 2 jalapenos, chopped
- 1 medium yellow onion, peeled and cut into chunks
- 4 cloves garlic
- 4 tbsp. extra virgin olive oil
- 2 cup chicken stock
- 2 cans green chilies
- 1 tbsp. cumin
- 1 tbsp. oregano
- ½ lime, juiced
- ¼ cup cilantro

*Directions:*

1. Place the pork shoulder chunks in a bowl and toss with flour -season with salt and pepper to taste.
2. Use desired traeger when cooking. Place a large cast-iron skillet on the bottom rack of the grill. Close the lid and preheat for 15 minutes.

3. Place the tomatillos, jalapeno, onion, and garlic on a sheet tray lined with foil and drizzle with two tbsp. olive oil - season with salt and pepper to taste.
4. Place the remaining olive oil in the heated cast iron skillet and cook the pork shoulder. Spread the meat evenly, then close.
5. Before closing the lid, place the vegetables in the tray on the grill rack. Close the lid of the grill.
6. Cook for 20 minutes without opening the lid or stirring the pork. After 20 minutes, remove the vegetables from the grill and transfer to a blender.
7. Pulse until smooth and pour into the pan with the pork. Stir in the chicken stock, green chilies, cumin, oregano, and lime juice, season with salt and pepper to taste. Close the grill lid and cook for another 20 minutes. Once cooked, stir in the cilantro.

*Nutritional Values (Per Serving):*

**Calories: 389**

Carbs: 4.5g
Fat: 24.3g
Protein: 28.5g
Sugar: 2.1g

Preparation time: 30 minute
Cooking time: 6 hours
Servings: **8 to 10**

*Ingredients:*

---

- 1 (3-pound) skinless pork belly (if not already skinned, use a sharp boning knife to remove the skin from the belly), cut into 1½- to 2-inch cube
- 1 batch Sweet Brown sugar Rub
- ½ cup honey
- 1 cup Bill's Best BBQ Sauce
- 2 tbsp. light brown sugar

*Directions:*

---

1. Supply your smoker with a traeger and follow the manufacturer's specific start-up procedure. Preheat the grill, with the lid closed, to 250°F.
2. Generously season the pork belly cubes with the rub. Using your hands, work the rub into the meat
3. Place the pork cubes directly on the grill grate and smoke until their internal temperature reaches 195°F.
4. Transfer the cubes from the grill to an aluminum pan. Add the honey, barbecue sauce, and brown sugar. Stir to combine and coat the pork.
5. Place the pan in the grill and smoke the pork for 1 hour, uncovered. Remove the pork from the grill and serve immediately.

*Nutritional Values (Per Serving):*

## Calories: 1301

Fat: 124g
Saturated Fat: 46g

## 3.7 - Zesty Herbal Smoke Pork Tenderloin

Preparation time: 30 minutes
Cooking time: 3 hours
Servings: **4**

*Ingredients:*

- 2–4 pork tenderloins
- 6 tbsp. BBQ sauce
- Pork Rub Ingredients:
- ½ cup cane sugar
- 1/3 tsp. chili powder
- ¼ tbsp. granulated onion
- ½ tbsp. granulated garlic
- 1 tbsp. dried chilies
- 1 tbsp. dill weed
- 1 tbsp. lemon powder
- 1 tbsp. mustard powder

*Directions:*

1. Take a large mixing bowl and combine all the poke rub ingredients in it.
2. Now preheat the smoker grill at 225°F until the smoke started to form
3. Cooking Time for 3 hours, until the internal temperature reaches 150°F.
4. After 3 hours a brush generous amount of the barbecue sauce and then left it to sit for 20 minutes before serving.
5. Serve and enjoy.

**Calories: 147**

Fat: 4 g
Protein: 26 g

Preparation time: 10 minutes
Cooking time: 45 minutes
Servings: **4**

*Ingredients:*

- 1 pack Pork sausages
- 1 pack Biscuit dough

*Directions:*

1. Preheat your traeger grill to 350°F.
2. Cut the sausages and the dough into thirds.
3. Wrap the dough around the sausages. Place them on a baking sheet.
4. Grill with a closed lid for 20–25 minutes or until they look cooked.
5. Take them out when they are golden brown.
6. Serve with a dip of your choice.

*Nutritional Values (Per Serving):*

**Calories: 0**

Cholesterol: 44 mg
Fat: 22 g
Protein: 9 g
Sodium: 732 mg

Preparation time: 20 minutes
Cooking time: 2 hours
Servings: **6**

*Ingredients:*

- 2 racks of St. Louis-style ribs
- 1 cup Traeger Pork and Poultry Rub
- ⅛ cup brown Sugar
- 4 tbsp. butter
- 4 tbsp. agave
- 1 bottle Traeger Sweet and Heat Barbecue Sauce

*Directions:*

1. Place the ribs on the working surface and remove the thin film of connective tissues covering it. In a smaller bowl, combine the Traeger Pork and Poultry Rub, brown sugar, butter, and agave. Mix until well combined.
2. Massage the rub onto the ribs and allow to rest in the fridge for at least 2 hours.
3. When ready to cook, fire the Traeger Grill to 225°F. Use desired traegers when cooking the ribs. Close the lid and preheat for 15 minutes.
4. Place the ribs on the grill grate and close the lid. Smoke for 1 hour and 30 minutes. Make sure to flip the ribs halfway through the cooking time.
5. Ten minutes before the cooking time ends, brush the ribs with Barbecue sauce.
6. Remove from the grill and allow to rest before slicing.

*Nutritional Values (Per Serving):*

## Calories: 399

Carbs: 3.5g
Fat: 20.5g
Protein: 47.2g
Sugar: 2.3g

### 3.10 - Smoked Baby Back Ribs

Preparation time: 20 minutes
Cooking time: 2 hours
Servings: **10**

*Ingredients:*

- 3 racks baby back ribs
- Salt and pepper to taste

*Directions:*

1. Clean the ribs by removing the extra membrane that covers them. Pat dry the ribs with a clean paper towel. Season the baby back ribs with salt and pepper to taste. Let rest in the fridge for at least 4 hours before cooking.
2. Once ready to cook, fire the Traeger Grill to 225°F. Use hickory traegers when cooking the ribs. Close the lid and preheat for 15 minutes.
3. Place the ribs on the grill grate and cook for two hours. Carefully flip the ribs halfway through the cooking time for even cooking.

*Nutritional Values (Per Serving):*

**Calories: 1037**

Carbs: 1.4g
Fat: 73.7g
Protein: 92.5g
Sugar: 0.2g

# Turkey, Rabbit and Veal

## 4.1 - BBQ Pulled Turkey Sandwiches

Preparation time: 30 minutes
Cooking time: 4 Hours
Servings: **1**

*Ingredients:*

- 6 skin-on turkey thighs
- 6 split and buttered buns
- 1 ½ cups of chicken broth
- 1 cup BBQ sauce
- Poultry rub

*Directions:*

1. Season the turkey thighs on both sides with poultry rub
2. Set the grill to preheat by pushing the temperature to 180°F
3. Arrange the turkey thighs on the grate of the grill and smoke them for 30 minutes
4. Now transfer the thighs to an aluminum foil which is disposable and then pour the brine right around the thighs
5. Cover it with a lid
6. Now increase the grill, temperature to 325°F and roast the thigh till the internal temperature reaches 180°F
7. Remove the foil from the grill but do not turn off the grill
8. Let the turkey thighs cool down a little
9. Now pour the dripping and serve
10. Remove the skin and discard it
11. Pull the meat into shreds and return it to the foil
12. Add 1 more cup of BBQ sauce and some more dripping

13. Now cover the foil with a lid and re-heat the turkey on the smoker for half an hour
14. Serve and enjoy

*Nutritional Values (Per Serving):*

**Calories: 390**

Carbs: 39 g
Cholesterol: 19 mg
Protein: 29 g
Sodium: 15 mg

Preparation time: 30 minutes
Cooking time: 6 Hours
Servings: **1**

*Ingredients:*

- 4 turkey legs
- 2 bay leaves
- 1 cup BBQ rubs
- 1 tbsp. crushed allspice berries
- 2 tsp. liquid smoke
- ½ gal cold water
- 4 cups ice
- 1 gal warm water
- ½ cup brown Sugar:
- ½ cup curing salt
- 1 tbsp. peppercorns, whole black

*Directions:*

1. Take a large stockpot and mix a gallon of warm water to curing salt, rub, peppercorns, brown sugar, liquid smoke, allspice, and bay leaves
2. Bring this mix to boil by keeping the flame on high heat and let all salt granules dissolve thoroughly
3. Now let it cool to room temperature
4. Now add ice and cold water and let the whole thing chill in the refrigerator
5. Add turkey legs and make sure they are submerged in the brine
6. Let it stay for a day

7. Now drain the turkey legs and get rid of the brine
8. Wash off the brine from the legs with the help of cold water and then pat it dry
9. Set the grill to preheat by keeping the temperature to 250°F
10. Lay the legs directly on the grate of the grill
11. Smoke it for 4 to 5 hours till the internal temperature reaches 165°F
12. Serve and enjoy

*Nutritional Values (Per Serving):*

**Calories: 410**

Carbs: 39 g
Cholesterol: 19 mg
Protein: 29 g
Sodium: 15 mg

Preparation time: 20 minutes
Cooking time: 3 hours 20 minutes
Servings: **8-12**

*Ingredients:*

- 1 turkey, neck
- 2 large Onion, eight
- 4 celeries, stalks
- 4 large carrots, fresh
- 8 clove garlic, smashed
- 8 thyme sprigs
- 4 cup chicken broth
- 1 tsp. chicken broth
- 1 tsp. salt
- 1 tsp. cracked black pepper
- 1 butter, sticks
- 1 cup all-purpose flour

*Directions:*

1. When ready to cook, set the temperature to 350°F and preheat the traeger grill with the lid closed, for 15 minutes.
2. Place turkey neck, celery, carrot (roughly chopped), garlic, onion, and thyme on a roasting pan. Add four cups of chicken stock then season with salt and pepper.
3. Move the prepped turkey on the rack into the roasting pan and place in the traeger grill.

4. Cook for about 3–4 hours until the breast reaches 160°F. The turkey will continue to cook and it will reach a finished internal temperature of 165°F.
5. Strain the drippings into a saucepan and simmer on low.
6. In a saucepan, mix butter (cut into 8 pieces) and flour with a whisk stirring until golden tan. This takes about 8 minutes, stirrings constantly.
7. Whisk the drippings into the roux then cook until it comes to a boil. Season with salt and pepper.

*Nutritional Values (Per Serving):*

**Calories: 160**

Carbohydrate: 27g
Fat: 23g
Protein: 55g
Saturated Fat: 6.1g

## 4.4 - Savory-Sweet Turkey Legs

Preparation time: 10 minutes
Cooking time: 5 hours
Servings: **4**

*Ingredients:*

- 1 gallon hot water
- 1 cup curing salt (such as Morton Tender Quick)
- ¼ cup packed light brown Sugar:
- 1 tsp. freshly ground black pepper
- 1 tsp. ground cloves
- 1 bay leaf
- 2 tsp. liquid smoke
- 4 turkey legs
- Mandarin Glaze, for serving

*Directions:*

1. In a huge container with a lid, stir together the water, curing salt, brown sugar, pepper, cloves, bay leaf, and liquid smoke until the salt and sugar are dissolved, let come to room temperature.
2. Submerge the turkey legs in the seasoned brine, cover, and refrigerate overnight.
3. When ready to smoke, remove the turkey legs from the brine and rinse them, discard the brine.
4. Supply your smoker with a traeger and follow the manufacturer's specific start-up procedure. Preheat, with the lid closed, to 225°F.
5. Arrange the turkey legs on the grill, close the lid, and smoke for 4 to 5 hours, or until dark brown and a meat

thermometer inserted in the thickest part of the meat reads 165°F.

6.  Serve with Mandarin Glaze on the side or drizzled over the turkey legs.

*Nutritional Values (Per Serving):*

**Calories: 190**

Carbs: 1g
Fat: 9g
Protein: 24g

## 4.5 - Spatchcock Smoked Turkey

Preparation time: 15 minutes
Cooking time: 4 hours 3 minutes
Servings: **6**

*Ingredients:*

- 1 (18 pounds) turkey
- 2 tbsp. finely chopped fresh parsley
- 1 tbsp. finely chopped fresh rosemary
- 2 tbsp. finely chopped fresh thyme
- ½ cup melted butter
- 1 tsp. garlic powder
- 1 tsp. onion powder
- 1 tsp. ground black pepper
- 2 tsp. salt or to taste
- 2 tbsp. finely chopped scallions

*Directions:*

1. Remove the turkey giblets and rinse the turkey, in and out, under cold running water.
2. Place the turkey on a working surface, breast side down. Use a poultry shear to cut the turkey along both sides of the backbone to remove the turkey's backbone.
3. Flip the turkey over, backside down. Now, press the turkey down to flatten it.
4. In a mixing bowl, combine the parsley, rosemary, scallions, thyme, butter, pepper, salt, and garlic and onion powder.
5. Rub butter mixture over all sides of the turkey.

6. Preheat your grill to HIGH (450°F) with the lid closed for 15 minutes.
7. Place the turkey directly on the grill grate and cook for 30 minutes. Reduce the heat to 300°F and cook for an additional 4 hours, or until the internal temperature of the thickest part of the thigh reaches 165°F.
8. Take out the turkey meat from the grill and let it rest for a few minutes. Cut into sizes and serve.

*Nutritional Values (Per Serving):*

**Calories: 780**

Carbs: 29.7g
Fat: 19g
Protein: 116.4g

# Game

## 5.1 - Quail on the Grill Marinated with Vinegar and Onions

Preparation time: 15 minutes
Cooking time: 1 ½ hour
Servings: **6**

*Ingredients:*

- 4 pcs. quail
  For the marinade:
- 2 pcs. onions
- 30 ml vinegar (9%)
- Salt to taste
- Ground black pepper, to taste
- 1 garlic clove

*Directions:*

1. Wash quail carcasses under running cold water, dry on paper towels, and put on a cutting board with the backup.
2. Using kitchen scissors, cut each quail along the back, unfold the ribs to the sides, and lay the carcass breast up. Beat the carcass lightly with a meat hammer (you can use the handle of a knife instead of a hammer).
3. For the marinade, peel and cut onions into several pieces. Fold in a blender and puree with a clove of garlic.
4. In a separate bowl, mix the vinegar with 50 ml of cold water.
5. Place the quail carcasses in a suitable bowl or food container, shifting with onion and garlic gruel, sprinkle with salt and pepper to taste. Stir it well so that the meat is well covered with the onion mass on all sides.

6. Pour diluted vinegar over the quail, stir, put a little oppression, and put in the refrigerator for at least 2-3 hours, or better overnight.
7. Burn firewood in the grill to the "gray" coals. Grease the sieve with vegetable oil, lay the quail carcasses, laying them out, as shown in the photo. Remember to shake off all the onions from them.
8. Bake over glowing coals, turning the wire rack from one side to the other from time to time. The quails on the wire rack are ready in about 20 minutes. Their readiness can be easily checked by piercing the breast with a knife: if clear juice flows out without impurities of blood, then the meat can be removed from the barbecue. Transfer the finished quails to a dish, cover with foil and let them rest for another 20 minutes.
9. Then you can serve it with fresh vegetables, herbs, and sauce to taste. Enjoy your meal!

*Nutritional Values (Per Serving):*

---

**Calories: 186**

Carbs: 21g
Fat: 10g
Fiber: 1.3 g
Protein: 11.1g

## 5.2 - Partridge with Cabbage

Preparation time: 15 minutes
Cooking time: 50 minutes
Servings: **4**

*Ingredients:*

- 1 kg white cabbage (1 small head cabbage)
- 2 partridges
- 200 g tea sausage
- 15 g smoked brisket
- 50 g butter
- 2 carrots
- 2 onions
- 2 carnation buds
- Salt
- Ground black pepper
- 15 g parsley
- Water

*Directions:*

1. Cut the head of cabbage into 4 parts. Remove the stump and thick ribs. Then immerse the cabbage in boiling salted water for 2 minutes. Then remove the cabbage from the boiling water, rinse with cold water, place the cabbage in a colander and let the water drain.
2. Brown the partridges in oil in a frying pan, then salt and pepper.
3. Put chopped cabbage and carrots, sprigs of greens, as well as 2 onions in a pressure cooker (or a roaster), in each of which first stick 1 clove bud.

4. After that, pour 125 g of boiling water into a pressure cooker (or roaster), add salt and pepper. Bring out the contents of the cooker to a boil with the lid open.
5. Place the sautéed partridge pieces in a pressure cooker (or roaster). Add finely chopped sausage and brisket there. Close the pressure cooker with a lid and simmer the partridges in the pressure cooker for 30 minutes and in the goose maker for 1 hour.

*Nutritional Values (Per Serving):*

**Calories: 187**

Carbs: 10g
Fat: 10g
Fiber: 1.3 g
Protein: 11.1g

## 5.3 - Tasty BBQ Ribs

Preparation time: 15 minutes
Cooking time: 4 hours
Servings: **8**

*Ingredients:*

- 2 ribs racks ribs
- 2 ½ tsp. brown Sugars:
- 1 ¼ tsp. instant coffees
- 1 ¼ tsp. kosher salt
- 1 ¼ tsp. garlic powder
- 1 ¼ tsp. coriander laces
- ¾ tsp. ground black pepper extra special
- ¼ tsp. cocoa powder
- 1 tsp. vegetable oil
- 1 ½ cups dry red wine
- 2 tbsp. canola oil
- 2 tbsp. chopped white onion
- 2 cups catsup sauce
- 1 ½ cups apple cider vinegar
- ¾ cup brown sugar
- 1 ½ tbsp. Maggi chicken broth
- 3 tbsp. Dijon mustard
- 2 tsp. chili powder
- 2 tsp. marinated chipotle chili sauce

*Directions:*

1. For the ribs:
2. Arrange the racks of ribs on a baking sheet with edges or inside a large roasting pan.

3. Using a knife, remove the membranes from the bone side of the ribs (this step is very important to make the ribs tender).
4. Dry the ribs with a paper towel, Place on the grill with the meat side facing up.
5. Combine the sugar, coffee granules, salt, garlic powder, coriander, pepper, and cocoa in the spice grinder, cover and process until smooth.
6. Lightly rub the ribs with oil.
7. Sprinkle with the mixture, pressing it gently to assist it to adhere to the ribs.
8. Let stand at room temperature for not more than 1 hour.
9. Preheat the oven to 250 F. Pour the beer into the bottom of the baking sheet.
10. Cover the bowl with foil, bake for 4 to 5 hours (this will be enough to make the meat tender, but it won't fall off the bones).
11. Prepare the BBQ sauce during the last 30 minutes of baking.
12. Preheat the grill. Grill the ribs over medium heat, turning once, for 5 minutes. Spread with sauce during roasting. Let the ribs stand for 10 minutes before serving.
13. For the BBQ sauce:
14. Heat the oil in a medium saucepan over medium heat.
15. Add onion, and then cook for 3 mins or until tender.
16. Add the catsup sauce, vinegar, sugar, and broth. Stir until the sugar and the broth dissolve.
17. Add mustard, chili powder, and marinade. Cover and cook for 30 minutes. The sauce will thicken as it simmers.

*Nutritional Values (Per Serving):*

**Calories: 203**

Carbs: 10g
Fat: 19g
Fiber: 1.3 g
Protein: 11.1g

## 5.4 - Filet Mignon with Bernese Sauce

Preparation time: 10 minutes
Cooking time: 45 minutes
Servings: **4**

*Ingredients:*

- 1/3 cup white vinegar
- 1/3 cup dry white wine
- 1 tsp. pepper
- 1 tsp. minced shallot
- 2 tsp. chopped parsley
- ¼ tsp. tarragon
- 3 pieces egg yolk
- 4 pieces beef fillet 2 cm thick
- 1 pinch salt

*Directions:*

1. Combine wine, vinegar, pepper, shallots, and tarragon, heat, and reduce to have 1/3 cup. Strain it and reserve.
2. Put a bowl on a water bath, the yolks, and the vinegar mixture and heat moving with a balloon whisk to begin to thicken, then put the parsley and remove from heat immediately and set aside.
3. Heat the grill and when it is very hot put a little oil and seal the fillets on the 2 sides, to brown a little, and put salt and pepper.
4. Once the steaks are well cooked. Serve immediately with the Bernese sauce.

*Nutritional Values (Per Serving):*

**Calories: 157**

Carbs: 10g
Fat: 10g
Fiber: 1.3 g
Protein: 11.1g

# Vegetables and Vegetarian

Preparation time: 10 minutes
Cooking time: 25 to 30 minutes
Servings: **3**

*Ingredients:*

- 1-pound fresh thick asparagus (15 to 20 spears)
- extra-virgin olive oil
- 5 slices thinly sliced bacon
- 1 tsp. Pete's Western Rub or salt and pepper

*Directions:*

1. Snap off the woody ends of asparagus and trim so they are all about the same length.
2. Divide the asparagus into bundles of 3 spears and spritz with olive oil. Wrap each bundle with 1 piece of bacon and then dust with the seasoning or salt and pepper to taste.
3. Configure your Traeger smoker-grill for indirect cooking, placing Teflon coated fiberglass mats on top of the grates (to prevent the asparagus from sticking to the grill grates). Preheat to 400°F using any type of Traegers. The grill can be preheated while prepping the asparagus.
4. Grill the bacon-wrapped asparagus for 25 to 30 minutes, until the asparagus is tender and the bacon is cooked and crispy.

*Nutritional Values (Per Serving):*

**Calories: 94**

Carbs: 5g
Fat: 7g
Protein: 4g

## 7.2 - Cinnamon Almonds

Preparation time: 15 minutes
Cooking time: 1 hour and 30 minutes
Servings: **4**

*Ingredients:*

- 1 pound almonds
- ½ cup granulated sugar
- ½ cup brown sugar
- 1 tbsp. cinnamon
- 1/8 tsp. salt
- 1 egg white

*Directions:*

1. In the meantime, take a small bowl, place egg white in it, and then whisk until frothy.
2. Add remaining ingredients for the seasoning in it, whisk until blended, then add almonds and toss until well coated.
3. Take a sheet pan and then spread almonds mixture in it.
4. When the grill has preheated, place a sheet pan containing almonds mixture on the grilling rack and grill for 90 minutes until almonds have roasted, stirring every 10 minutes.
5. Check the fire after one hour of smoking and add more wood pallets if required.
6. When done, remove the sheet pan from the grill, let it cool slightly and then serve.

## Nutritional Values (Per Serving):

**Calories: 136.9**

Carbs: 15g
Fat: 8g
Protein: 3g

Preparation time: 30 minutes
Cooking time: 45 minutes
Servings: **4**

*Ingredients:*

---

For the Smoked Hummus:
- 1 ½ cups cooked chickpeas
- 1 tbsp. minced garlic
- 1 tsp. salt
- 4 tbsp. lemon juice
- 2 tbsp. olive oil
- 1/3 cup tahini

For the Vegetables:
- 2 large Portobello mushrooms
- 1 small eggplant, destemmed, sliced into strips
- 1 tsp. salt
- 1 small zucchini, trimmed, sliced into strips
- ½ tsp. ground black pepper
- 1 small yellow squash, peeled, sliced into strips ¼ cup olive oil

For the Cheese:
- 1 lemon, juiced
- ½ tsp. minced garlic
- ¼ tsp. ground black pepper
- ¼ tsp. salt
- ½ cup ricotta cheese

To Assemble:
- 1 bunch basil, leaves chopped
- 2 heirloom tomatoes, sliced
- 4 ciabatta buns, halved

1. Switch on the Traeger grill, fill the grill hopper with pecan flavored Traegers, power the grill on by using the control panel, select 'smoke' on the temperature dial, or set the temperature to 180°F and let it preheat for a minimum of 15 minutes.
2. Meanwhile, prepare the hummus, and for this, take a sheet tray and spread chickpeas on it.
3. When the grill has preheated, open the lid, place the sheet tray on the grill grate, shut the grill, and smoke for 20 minutes.
4. When done, transfer chickpeas to a food processor, add remaining ingredients for the hummus in it, and pulse for 2 minutes until smooth, set aside until required.
5. Change the smoking temperature to 500°F, shut with lid, and let it preheat for 10 minutes.
6. Meanwhile, prepare vegetables and for this, take a large bowl, place all the vegetables in it, add salt and black pepper, drizzle with oil and lemon juice and toss until coated.
7. Place vegetables on the grill grate, shut with lid, and then smoke for eggplant, zucchini, and squash for 15 minutes and mushrooms for 25 minutes.
8. Meanwhile, prepare the cheese and for this, take a small bowl, place all of its ingredients in it and stir until well combined.
9. Assemble the sandwich for this, cut buns in half lengthwise, spread prepared hummus on one side, spread cheese on the other side, then stuff with grilled vegetables and top with tomatoes and basil.
10. Serve straight away.

*Nutritional Values (Per Serving):*

---

**Calories: 560**

Carbs: 45 g
Fat: 40 g
Fiber: 6.8 g
Protein: 8.3 g

## 7.4 - Smoked Broccoli

Preparation time: 10 minutes
Cooking time: 30 minutes
Servings: **4**

*Ingredients:*

- 2 heads broccoli
- Kosher salt
- 2 tbsp. vegetable oil
- Fresh Pepper (ground)

*Directions:*

1. Preheat your smoker to 350°F.
2. Separate the florets from the heads.
3. Coat the broccoli with vegetable oil by tossing. Thereafter, season with salt and pepper.
4. Using a grilling basket put the broccoli on the grate of the smoker and smoke for 30 minutes or till crisp.
5. Enjoy!

*Nutritional Values (Per Serving):*

**Calories: 76**

Carbs: 3.1g
Fat: 7g
Protein: 1.3g
Saturated Fat: 1.3g

## 7.5 - Traeger Grilled Asparagus and Honey Glazed Carrots

Preparation time: 15 minutes
Cooking time: 35 minutes
Servings: **5**

*Ingredients:*

- 1 bunch asparagus, trimmed ends
- 1 lb. carrots, peeled
- 2 tbsp. olive oil
- Sea salt to taste
- 2 tbsp. honey
- Lemon zest

*Directions:*

1. Sprinkle the asparagus with oil and sea salt. Drizzle the carrots with honey and salt.
2. Preheat the Traeger to 165°F with the lid closed for 15 minutes.
3. Place the carrots in the Traeger and cook for 15 minutes. Add asparagus and cook for 20 more minutes or until cooked through.
4. Top the carrots and asparagus with lemon zest. Enjoy.

## Calories: 1680

Carbs: 10g
Fat: 30g
Net Carbs: 10g
Protein: 4g
Saturated Fat: 2g
Sodium: 514mg

## 7.6 - Smoked Potatoes

Preparation time: 30 minutes
Cooking time: 2 hours
Servings: **4**

*Ingredients:*

- 1.5 lb. potatoes (gemstone)
- Fresh parsley (chopped)
- ¼ cup Parmesan (grated)
- Marinade Ingredients:
- 6 cloves garlic (minced)
- 2 tbsp. olive oil
- ½ tsp. dried dill
- ½ tsp. basil (dried)
- ½ tsp. oregano (dried)
- ½ tsp. Italian seasoning (dried)
- ¼ tsp. fresh pepper (ground)
- ½ tsp. kosher salt

*Directions:*

1. The initial step is rinsing the potatoes with water. When done, place the potatoes in a large Ziploc bag.
2. In a mixing bowl, add and combine the minced garlic cloves, dill, Italian seasoning, basil, and ground pepper. Add this mixture to the Ziploc bag together with the potatoes.
3. Coat the potatoes by shaking the Ziploc bag and refrigerate for 2 hours.
4. Once ready to cook, preheat your smoker to 225F.

5. Use aluminum foil to make a foil packet and place it in the potatoes.
6. Pour in two tbsp. of water in the foil and fold it in half on its edges.
7. Put the foil packet on the smoker rack and smoke for 2 hours.
8. Remove from the smoker and top with the grated parmesan and parsley.

*Nutritional Values (Per Serving):*

### Calories: 210

Carbs: 28.9g
Cholesterol: 5mg
Fat: 8.9g
Fiber: 4.3g
Protein: 5.5g
Saturated Fat: 2.1
Sodium: 368mg
Sugar: 2.1g

## 7.7 - Smoked Deviled Eggs

Preparation time: 15 minutes
Cooking time: 30 minutes
Servings: **5**

*Ingredients:*

- 7 hard-boiled eggs, peeled
- 3 tbsp. mayonnaise
- 3 tbsp. chives, diced
- 1 tbsp. brown mustard
- 1 tbsp. apple cider vinegar
- Dash hot sauce
- Salt and pepper
- 2 tbsp. cooked bacon, crumbled
- Paprika to taste

*Directions:*

1. Preheat the Traeger to 180°F for 15 minutes with the lid closed.
2. Place the eggs on the grill grate and smoke the eggs for 30 minutes. Remove the eggs from the grill and let cool.
3. Half the eggs and scoop the egg yolks into a Ziploc bag.
4. Add all other ingredients in the Ziploc bag except bacon and paprika. Mix until smooth.
5. Pipe the mixture into the egg whites then top with bacon and paprika.
6. Let rest then serve and enjoy.

*Nutritional Values (Per Serving):*

**Calories: 140**

Carbs: 1g
Fat: 12g
Fiber: 0g
Net Carbs: 1g
Potassium: 100mg
Protein: 6g
Saturated Fat: 3g
Sodium: 210mg
Sugar: 0g

# Fish and Seafood

127

Preparation time: 7 hours
Cooking time: 3 hours
Servings: **8**

*Ingredients:*

---

- 4 pounds trout fillets
- ½ cup salt
- ½ cup brown sugar
- 2 quarts water

*Directions:*

---

1. Pour water into a large container with a lid, add salt and sugar and stir until salt and sugar are dissolved completely.
2. Add trout, pour in more water to submerge trout in brine, and refrigerate for 4 to 8 hours, covering the container.
3. Then remove trout from brine, rinse well and pat dry with paper towels.
4. Place trout on a cooling rack, skin side down, and cool in the refrigerator for 2 hours or until dry.
5. Then remove trout from the refrigerator and bring to room temperature.
6. In the meantime, plug in the smoker, fill its tray with maple woodchips and water pan halfway through and place the dripping pan above the water pan.
7. Then open the top vent, shut with lid, and use temperature settings to preheat the smoker at 160°F.
8. In the meantime,

9. Place trout on smoker rack, insert a meat thermometer, then shut with lid and set the timer to smoke for 2 ½ to 3 hours or more until meat thermometer registers an internal temperature of 145°F.
10. Check vent of smoker every hour and add more woodchips and water to maintain temperature and smoke.
11. Serve straight away.

*Nutritional Values (Per Serving):*

**Calories: 49**

Carbs: 0 g
Fat: 1.2 g
Fiber: 0 g
Protein: 8.8 g

Preparation time: 15 minutes
Cooking time: 30 minutes
Servings: **8**

*Ingredients:*

- 2 lbs. squid
- 4 cloves garlic
- 10 sprigs parsley
- 4 slices old bread
- 1/3 cup milk
- Salt and ground white pepper
- 4 slices prosciutto
- 4 slices cheese
- 3 tbsp. olive oil
- 1 lemon

*Directions:*

1. Wash and clean your squid and pat dry on a paper towel. Finely chop parsley and garlic.
2. Cut bread into cubes and soak it in milk.
3. Add parsley, garlic, white pepper, and salt. Stir well together.
4. Cut the cheese into larger pieces (the pieces should be large enough that they can be pushed through the opening of the squid).
5. Mix the cheese with prosciutto slices and stir well together with the remaining ingredients.

6. Use your fingers to open the bag pack of squid and pushed the mixture inside. At the end add some more bread.
7. Close the openings with toothpicks.
8. Start your Traeger grill on smoke with the lid open for 5 minutes.
9. Set the temperature to the highest setting and preheat, lid closed, for 10- 15 minutes.
10. Grill squid for 3 – 4 minutes being careful not to burn the squid. Serve hot.

*Nutritional Values (Per Serving):*

**Calories: 290**

Carbs: 13g
Cholesterol: 288mg
Fat: 13g
Protein: 25g

Preparation time: 10 minutes
Cooking time: 30 minutes
Servings: **4**

*Ingredients:*

- 4 Yellowtail Filets (6 oz.)
- 1 lb. new Potatoes
- 2 tbsp. Olive oil
- 1 lb. Mushrooms, oyster
- 1 tsp. ground Black pepper
- 4 tbsp. olive oil

*Directions:*

1. Preheat the grill to high with a closed lid.
2. Place an iron pan directly on the grill. Let it heat for 10 minutes.
3. Rub the fish with oil. Season with black pepper and salt.
4. In 2 different bowls place the mushrooms and potatoes, drizzle with oil, and season with black pepper and salt. Toss.
5. Place the potatoes in the pan. Cook 10 minutes. Add the mushrooms.
6. Place the fillets on the grate with the skin down. Cook for 6 minutes and flip. Cook for 4 minutes more.
7. While the potatoes, mushrooms, and fish are cooking make the Salsa Verde. In a bowl combine all the ingredients and stir to combine.
8. Place the mushrooms and potatoes on a plate, top with a fillet, and drizzle with the Salsa Verde.

9. Serve and Enjoy!

*Nutritional Values (Per Serving):*

**Calories: 398**

Carbs: 20g
Fat: 18gg
Protein: 52g

Preparation time: 15 minutes
Cooking time: 15 minutes
Servings: **2**

*Ingredients:*

- 2 tbsp. vegetable oil and more for the grill
- 12 large sea scallops, side muscle removed Kosher salt and ground black pepper Lemony Salsa Verde

*Directions:*

1. Set up the grill for medium-high heat, then oil the grate. Toss the scallops with 2 tbsp. of oil on a rimmed baking sheet and season with salt and pepper.
2. Utilizing a fish spatula or your hands, place the scallops on the grill.
3. Grill them, occasionally turning, until gently colored and cooked through, around 2 minutes for each side.
4. Serve the scallops with Lemony Salsa Verde.

*Nutritional Values (Per Serving):*

**Calories: 30**

Carbs: 1g
Cholesterol: 17mg
Fat: 1g
Protein: 6g

Preparation time: 20 minutes
Cooking time: 25 minutes
Servings: **8**

*Ingredients:*

- 1 jar (28oz.) Crushed Tomatoes
- 2 oz. Tomato paste
- ¼ cup White wine
- ¼ cup Chicken Stock
- 2 tbsp. Butter
- 2 Garlic cloves, minced
- ¼ Onion, diced
- ½ lb. Shrimp divined and cleaned
- ½ lb. Clams
- ½ lb. Halibut
- Parsley
- Bread

*Directions:*

1. Preheat the grill to 300°F with a closed lid.
2. Place a Dutch oven over medium heat and melt the butter.
3. Sauté the onion for 4 - 7 minutes. Add the garlic. Cook for 1 more minute.
4. Add the tomato paste. Cook until the color becomes rust red. Pour the stock and wine. Cook 10 minutes. Add the tomatoes, simmer.

5. Chop the halibut and together with the other seafood add in the Dutch oven. Place it on the grill and cover with a lid.
6. Let it cook for 20 minutes.
7. Season with black pepper and salt and set aside.
8. Top with chopped parsley and serve with bread.
9. Enjoy!

*Nutritional Values (Per Serving):*

**Calories: 188**

Carbs: 7g
Fat: 12g
Protein: 25g

Preparation time: 45 minutes
Cooking time: 10 minutes
Servings: **4**

*Ingredients:*

- 3 tbsp. olive oil
- 6 cloves garlic
- 2 tbsp. chicken dry rub
- 6 oz. chili
- 1 ½ tbsp. white vinegar
- 1 ½ tsp. sugar
- 6 lb. shrimp, peeled and deveined

*Directions:*

1. Add olive oil, garlic, dry rub, chili, vinegar, and sugar in a food processor.
2. Blend until smooth.
3. Transfer mixture to a bowl.
4. Stir in shrimp.
5. Cover and refrigerate for 30 minutes.
6. Preheat the Traeger grill to hit for 15 minutes while the lid is closed.
7. Thread shrimp onto skewers.
8. Grill for 3 minutes per side.
9. Serving suggestion: Garnish with chopped herbs.

*Nutritional Values (Per Serving):*

## Calories: 250

Carbs: 18g
Fat: 13g
Fiber: 0g
Protein: 24g

Preparation time: 30 minutes
Cooking time: 1h 30 minutes
Servings: **8 - 12**

*Ingredients:*

- 3 lb. Shrimp (large), with tails, divided
- 2 lb. Kielbasa Smoked Sausage
- 6 corns cut into 3 pieces
- 2 lb. Potatoes, red
- Old Bay

*Directions:*

1. Preheat the grill to 275F with a closed lid.
2. First, cook the sausage on the grill. Cook for 1 hour.
3. Increase the temperature to high. Season the corn and potatoes with Old Bay. Now roast until they become tender.
4. Season the shrimp with the Old Bay and cook on the grill for 20 minutes.
5. In a bowl combine the cooked ingredients. Toss.
6. Adjust seasoning with Old Bay and serve. Enjoy!

*Nutritional Values (Per Serving):*

**Calories: 530**

Carbs: 32g
Fat: 35g
Fiber: 1g
Protein: 20g

# Cheese and Breads

## 10.1 - Traeger-Grill Flatbread Pizza

Preparation time: 10 minutes
Cooking time: 20 minutes
Servings: **3**

*Ingredients:*

Dough :
- 2 cups flour
- 1 tbsp. salt
- 1 tbsp. sugar
- 2 tbsp. yeast
- 6 oz. warm water
Toppings :
- Green/red bell pepper
- ½ garlic
- zucchini
- ½ onion
- Olive oil
- 5 bacon strips
- 1 cup halved yellow cherry tomatoes
- Sliced jalapenos
- Sliced green olives
- Sliced Kalamata olives
- Goat cheese
- For drizzling: Balsamic vinegar

1. Combine all dough ingredients in a stand mixer bowl. Mix until the dough is smooth and elastic. Divide into 3 equal balls.
2. Roll each dough ball with a rolling pin into a thin round enough to fit a 12-inch skillet.
3. Grease the skillet using olive oil.
4. Meanwhile, turn your Traeger grill on smoke for about 4-5 minutes with the lid open. Turn to high and preheat for about 10-15 minutes with the lid closed.
5. Once ready, arrange peppers, garlic, zucchini, and onion on the grill grate then drizzle with oil and salt. Check at 10 minutes.
6. Now remove zucchini from the grill and add bacon. Continue to cook for another 10 minutes until bacon is done.
7. Transfer the toppings to a chopping board to cool. Chop tomatoes, jalapenos, and olive.
8. Brush your crust with oil and smash garlic with a fork over the crust. Smear carefully not to tear the crust.
9. Add toppings to the crust in the skillet.
10. Place the skillet on the grill and cook for about 20 minutes until brown edges.
11. Repeat for the other crusts.
12. Now drizzle each with vinegar and slice.
13. Serve and enjoy.

## Calories: 342

Carbs: 70.7g
Fat: 1.2g
Fiber: 3.9g
Net Carbs: 66.8g
Potassium: 250mg
Protein: 11.7g
Saturated Fat: 0.2g
Sodium: 2333mg
Sugar: 4.2g

## 10.2 - Smoked Cheddar Cheese

Preparation time: 5 minutes
Cooking time: 5 hour
Servings: **2**

*Ingredients:*

---

- 2, 8-oz, cheddar cheese blocks

*Directions:*

---

1. Preheat and set your Traeger grill to 90°F.
2. Place the cheese blocks directly on the grill grate and smoke for about 4 hours.
3. Remove and transfer into a plastic bag, resealable. Refrigerate for about 2 weeks to allow flavor from smoke to permeate your cheese.
4. Now enjoy!

*Nutritional Values (Per Serving):*

---

**Calories: 115**

Carbs: 0.9g
Fat: 9.5g
Fiber: 0g
Net Carbs: 0.9g
Potassium: 79mg
Protein: 6.5g
Saturated Fat: 5.4g
Sodium: 185mg
Sugar: 0.1g

## 10.3 - Grilled Peaches and Cream

Preparation time: 15 minutes
Cooking time: 8 minutes
Servings: **8**

*Ingredients:*

- 4 halved and pitted peaches
- 1 tbsp. vegetable oil
- 2 tbsp. clover honey
- 1 cup cream cheese, soft with honey and nuts

*Directions:*

1. Preheat your Traeger grill to medium-high heat.
2. Coat the peaches lightly with oil and place on the grill pit side down.
3. Grill for about 5 minutes until nice grill marks on the surfaces.
4. Turn over the peaches then drizzle with honey.
5. Spread and cream cheese dollop where the pit was and grill for additional 2-3 minutes until the filling becomes warm.
6. Serve immediately.

*Nutritional Values (Per Serving):*

## Calories: 139

Carbs: 11.6g
Fat: 10.2g
Fiber: 0g
Net Carbs: 11.6g
Potassium: 19mg
Protein: 1.1g
Saturated Fat: 5g
Sodium: 135mg
Sugar: 12g

# Nut, Fruits and Dessert

## 11.1 - Pineapple Cake

Preparation time: 30 minutes
Cooking time: 1 hour and 20 minutes
Servings: **8**

*Ingredients:*

- 1 cup sugar
- 1 tbsp. baking powder
- 1 cup buttermilk
- ½ tsp. salt
- 1 jar maraschino cherries
- 1 stick butter, divided
- ¾ cup brown sugar
- 1 can pineapple slices
- 1 ½ cup flour

*Directions:*

1. Add Traegers to your smoker and follow your cooker's startup procedure. Preheat your smoker, with your lid closed, until it reaches 350.
2. Take a medium-sized cast iron skillet, melt one half stick butter. Be sure to coat the entire skillet. Sprinkle brown sugar into a cast iron skillet.
3. Lay the sliced pineapple on top of the brown sugar. Put a cherry into each individual pineapple ring.
4. Mix together the salt, baking powder, flour, and sugar. Add in the eggs, one-half stick melted butter and buttermilk. Whisk to combine.
5. Put the cake on the grill and cook for an hour.

6. Take off from the grill and let it sit for ten minutes. Flip onto a serving platter.

*Nutritional Values (Per Serving):*

**Calories: 120**

Carbs: 18g
Fat: 5g
Fiber: 0g
Protein: 1g

Preparation time: 20 minutes
Cooking time: 35-45 minutes
Servings: **4**

*Ingredients:*

- 4barely ripe peaches, halved and pitted
- 1tbsp. firmly packed brown sugar
- 1-pint vanilla ice cream
- 3tbsp. honey

*Directions:*

1. Preheat your smoker to 200°F
2. Sprinkle cut peach halves with brown sugar
3. Transfer them to smoker and smoke for 33-45 minutes
4. Transfer the peach halves to dessert plates and top with vanilla ice cream
5. Drizzle honey and serve!

*Nutritional Values (Per Serving):*

**Calories: 309**

Carbs: 17g
Fats: 27g
Fiber: 2g

# Lamb

## 12.1 - Lamb Chops

Preparation time: 10 minutes
Cooking time: 10 minutes
Servings: **8**

*Ingredients:*

---

For the Lamb:
- 16 lamb chops, fat trimmed
- 2 tbsp. Greek Freak seasoning
For the Mint Sauce:
- 1 tbsp. chopped parsley
- 12 cloves garlic, peeled
- 1 tbsp. chopped mint
- ¼ tsp. dried oregano
- 1 tsp. salt
- ¼ tsp. ground black pepper
- ¾ cup lemon juice
- 1 cup olive oil

*Directions:*

---

1. Prepare the mint sauce and for this, place all of its ingredients in a food processor and then pulse for 1 minute until smooth.
2. Pour 1/3 cup of the mint sauce into a plastic bag, add lamb chops in it, seal the bag, turn it upside to coat lamb chops with the sauce and then let them marinate for a minimum of 30 minutes in the refrigerator.
3. When ready to cook, switch on the Traeger grill, fill the grill hopper with apple-flavored Traegers, power the grill on by using the control panel, select 'smoke' on the

temperature dial, or set the temperature to 450°F and let it preheat for a minimum of 15 minutes.

4. Meanwhile, remove lamb chops from the marinade and then season with Greek seasoning.
5. When the grill has preheated, open the lid, place lamb chops on the grill grate, shut the grill, and smoke for 4 to 5 minutes per side until cooked to the desired level.
6. When done, transfer the lamb chops to a dish and then serves.

*Nutritional Values (Per Serving):*

**Calories: 362**

Carbs: 0 g
Fat: 26 g
Fiber: 0 g
Protein: 31 g

## 12.2 - Classic Lamb Chops

Preparation time: 10 minutes
Cooking time: 30 minutes
Servings: **4**

*Ingredients:*

- Traeger Flavor: Alder
- 4 (8-ounce) bone-in lamb chops
- 2 tbsp. olive oil
- 1 batch Rosemary-Garlic Lamb Seasoning

*Directions:*

1. Supply your smoker with Traeger and follow the manufacturer's specific start-up procedure. Preheat the grill to 350°F. Close the lid
2. Rub the lamb generously with olive oil and coat them on both sides with the seasoning.
3. Put the chops directly on the grill grate and grill until their internal temperature reaches 145°F. Remove the lamb from the grill and serve immediately.

*Nutritional Values (Per Serving):*

**Calories: 50**

Carbs: 4g
Fat: 2.5g
Fiber: 2g
Protein: 2g

## 12.3 - Simple Traeger Grilled Lamb Chops

Preparation time: 10 Minutes
Cooking time: 20 Minutes
Servings: **6**

*Ingredients:*

- ¼ cup white vinegar, distilled
- 2 tbsp. olive oil
- 2 tbsp. salt
- ½ tbsp. black pepper
- 1 tbsp. minced garlic
- 1 onion, thinly sliced
- 2 lb. lamb chops

*Directions:*

1. In a resealable bag, mix vinegar, oil, salt, black pepper, garlic, and sliced onions until all salt has dissolved.
2. Add the lamb and toss until evenly coated. Place in a fridge to marinate for 2 hours.
3. Preheat your Traeger.
4. Remove the lamb from the resealable bag and leave any onion that is stuck on the meat. Use an aluminum foil to cover any exposed bone ends.
5. Grill until the desired doneness is achieved. Serve and enjoy when hot.

## Nutritional Values (Per Serving):

**Calories: 519**

Carbs: 2.3g
Fat: 44.8g
Fiber: 0.4g
Potassium: 358.6mg
Protein: 25g
Sodium: 861mg
Sugar: 0.8g

# Appetizers and Sides

Preparation time: 5 Minutes
Cooking time: 20 Minutes
Servings: **4**

*Ingredients:*

---

- 1 ½ tbsp. olive oil
- 1 ½ tsp. red wine vinegar
- ¼ tsp. Dijon mustard
- 1/8 tsp. salt
- 1/8 tsp. pepper
- 5 cups mixed baby greens
- ½ cup raspberries
- ¼ cup chopped toasted pecans
- 1-ounce blue cheese

*Directions:*

---

1. Join olive oil, vinegar, Dijon mustard, salt, and pepper.
2. Include blended infant greens, too.
3. Top with raspberries, walnuts, and blue cheddar.

*Nutritional Values (Per Serving):*

---

**Calories: 133**

Fat: 12.2g
Sodium: 193mg

Preparation time: 30 minutes
Cooking time: 15 minutes
Servings: **6-10 (1-2 sliders each as an appetizer)**

*Ingredients:*

- 1-pound ground beef (80% lean)
- ½ tsp. garlic salt
- ½ tsp. salt
- ½ tsp. garlic
- ½ tsp. onion
- ½ tsp. black pepper
- 6 bacon slices, cut in half
- ½cup mayonnaise
- 2 tsp. creamy wasabi (optional)
- 6 (1 oz.) sliced sharp cheddar cheese, cut in half (optional)
- Sliced red onion
- ½ cup sliced kosher dill pickles
- 12 mini pieces bread sliced horizontally
- Ketchup

*Directions:*

1. Place ground beef, garlic salt, seasoned salt, garlic powder, onion powder, and black pepper in a medium bowl.
2. Divide the meat mixture into 12 equal parts, shape into small thin round patties (about 2 ounces each) and save.
3. Cook the bacon on medium heat over medium heat for 5-8 minutes until crunchy. Set aside.

4. To make the sauce, mix the mayonnaise and horseradish in a small bowl.

5. Set up a Traeger smoker grill for direct cooking to use griddle accessories. Contact the manufacturer to see if there is a griddle accessory that works with the wooden Traeger smoker grill.

6. Spray a cooking spray on the griddle cooking surface for best non-stick results.

7. Preheat Traeger smoker grill to 350°F using selected Traegers. The griddle surface should be approximately 400°F.

8. Grill the putty for 3-4 minutes each until the internal temperature reaches 160°F.

9. If necessary, place a sharp cheddar cheese slice on each patty while the patty is on the griddle or after the patty is removed from the griddle. Place a small amount of mayonnaise mixture, a slice of red onion, and a hamburger pate in the lower half of each roll. Pickled slices, bacon, and ketchup.

*Nutritional Values (Per Serving):*

**Calories: 379**

Carbs: 11g
Fat: 21g
Protein: 25g

## 13.3 - Roasted Tomatoes

Preparation time: 10 Minutes
Cooking time: 3 Hours
Servings: **2 to 4**

*Ingredients:*

* 3 ripe Tomatoes, large
* 1 tbsp. black pepper
* 2 tbsp. Salt
* 2 tsp. Basil
* 2 tsp. Sugar
* Oil

*Directions:*

1. Place parchment paper on a baking sheet. Preheat the grill to 225F with a closed lid.
2. Remove the stems from the tomatoes. Cut them into slices (½ inch).
3. In a bowl combine the basil, sugar, pepper, and salt. Mix well.
4. Pour oil on a plate. Dip the tomatoes (just one side) in the oil.
5. Dust each slice with the mixture.
6. Grill the tomatoes for 3 hours.
7. Serve and enjoy! (You can serve it with mozzarella pieces).

## Nutritional Values (Per Serving):

**Calories: 40**

Carbs: 2g
Fat: 3g
Protein: 1g

Preparation time: 10 Minutes
Cooking time: 25 Minutes
Servings: **2 to 4**

*Ingredients:*

- 1 tbsp. Fennel, ground
- ½ cup Brown Sugar
- 1 lb. Slab Bacon, cut into cubes (1 inch)
- 1 tsp. Black pepper
- Salt

*Directions:*

1. Take an aluminum foil and then fold in half.
2. Preheat the grill to 350°F with a closed lid.
3. In a bowl combine the black pepper, salt, fennel, and sugar. Stir.
4. Place the pork in the seasoning mixture. Toss to coat. Transfer on the foil.
5. Place the foil on the grill. Bake for 25 minutes, or until crispy and bubbly.
6. Serve and enjoy!

*Nutritional Values (Per Serving):*

**Calories: 300**

Carbs: 4g
Fat: 36g
Protein: 27g

# Traditional

## 14.1 - Chicken Casserole

Preparation time: 15 minutes
Cooking time: 55 minutes
Servings: **8**

*Ingredients:*

---

- 2 (15-ounce) cans cream of chicken soup
- 2 cups milk
- 2 tbsp. unsalted butter
- ¼ cup all-purpose flour
- 1 pound skinless, boneless chicken thighs, chopped ½ cup hatch chiles, chopped
- 2 medium onions, chopped
- 1 tbsp. fresh thyme, chopped
- Salt and ground black pepper, as required 1 cup cooked bacon, chopped 1 cup tater tots

*Directions:*

---

1. Preheat the Traeger grill & Smoker on grill setting to 400°F.
2. In a large bowl, mix together chicken soup and milk.
3. In a skillet, melt butter over medium heat.
4. Slowly, add flour and cook for about 1-2 minutes or until smooth, stirring continuously.
5. Slowly, add soup mixture, beating continuously until smooth.
6. Cook until the mixture starts to thicken, stirring continuously.
7. Stir in remaining ingredients except for bacon and simmer for about 10-15 minutes.

8. Stir in bacon and transfer mixture into a 2½-quart casserole dish.
9. Place tater tots on top of the casserole evenly.
10. Arrange the pan onto the grill and cook for about 30-35 minutes.
11. Serve hot.

*Nutritional Values (Per Serving):*

**Calories: 440**

Carbs: 22.2 g
Cholesterol: 86 mg
Fat: 25.8 g
Fiber: 1.5 g
Protein: 28.9 g
Saturated Fat: 9.3 g
Sodium: 1565 mg
Sugar: 4.6 g

## 14.2 - Premium Salmon Nuggets

Preparation time: 20 minutes +marinate time
Cooking time: 1-2 hours
Servings: **8**

*Ingredients:*

- 3 cups of packed brown Sugar:
- 1 cup of salt
- 1 tbsp. of onion, minced
- 2 tsp. of chipotle seasoning
- 2 tsp. of fresh ground black pepper
- 1 garlic clove, minced
- 1-2 pound of salmon fillets, cut up into bite-sized portions

*Directions:*

1. Take a large-sized bowl and stir in brown Sugar:, salt, chipotle seasoning, onion, garlic and pepper
2. Transfer salmon to a large shallow marinating dish
3. Pour dry marinade over fish and cover, refrigerate overnight
4. Take your drip pan and add water, cover with aluminum foil. Pre-heat your smoker to 180°F
5. Use water fill water pan halfway through and place it over drip pan. Add wood chips to the side tray
6. Rinse the salmon chunks thoroughly and remove salt
7. Transfer them to grill rack and smoke for 1-2 hours
8. Remove the heat and enjoy it!

*Nutritional Values (Per Serving):*

## Calories: 120

Carbs: 3g
Fats: 18g
Fiber: 2g

# Conclusion

# Final Thoughts

Traeger grills offer a revolutionary solution to the cooking problems, and promise to change how we cook forever.

In modern society, Traeger grills are available in various types of models and designs to cater for different needs.

A great option for those who want to have more of a hassle-free cooking experience.

With the thermostat app's detailed recipes and ability to remotely monitor your burner settings, you're less likely to burn food while trying to cook.

Whether you're hosting a backyard cookout for friends or preparing food for competitions, Traeger grills can enable you to make meals with less effort and give your dishes an unmatched flavor.

Although Traegers grill isn't everyone's favorite choice, it is a must-have outdoor appliance. Whether you love smoking, grilling, roasting or directly cooking food the Traeger grill can be adjusted to fit any of your needs.

Cooking with a Traeger grill allows you to choose the desired flavor of meat, vegetables, and other ingredients. Each type has its own personality and taste so it's easy to create your own signature meal!

There are some perks to using the Traegers, but one must be willing to try.

There are many ways to cook food, but smoke can be one of the most popular methods. It is a process that takes a long time and low temperature which thoroughly cooks the meat. Smoke enhances flavor better than other cooking techniques and preserves nutrients infinitely.

The art of smoking is not an easy one to pick up and master - it can take 6 months or more, but new smokers are rewarded with a wide variety of smoked meat flavors that will make anyone drool.

Because of the many smoking techniques, you have to experiment with different smoking method and different types of woods. You can kind of trial and error your way towards a technique that is ideal for your temperament and style. Try cooking meat products for several hours using a heat source not directly on the meat. But make sure there's plenty of space so smoke can soak your meat and have a way to go out.

The picture of a good time with loved ones, neighbors, and friends having a backyard party or barbecue is indeed pretty to look at. Having some recipes you can prepare in your grill smoker will make the company stay for more than just 4 or 5 beers.

The Traeger smoker-grill offers hundreds of recipes that you can experiment with, improve, or make your own. Whether you want to use one of the proven and tested cookbooks or try something new, it is up to you. You will easily find recipes that are well-received by others and also have a delicious taste.

One of the great things about these recipes is that they are easy to prepare. Simply by following a few simple steps and having the right ingredients at your disposal, you can make delicious meals in no time!

When buying a Traeger grill, there are quite a few factors to consider, like the services offered and whether it's suitable for your needs. With new models being produced each year, you need to shop smartly so that you buy the right one for you.

It's important to know what types of grill are trending and which ones will suit your needs best. You want a grilling product that has reliable technology in design, and if you don't upgrade your purchase then you might be stuck with an outdated product.

The Traeger is a perfect personal grill for anyone who wants to make their food taste better and cooking easier.

You no longer have to search the internet for your favorite Traeger Smoker Grill recipes. This book is a comprehensive solution designed to eliminate all of your struggles when it comes finding the perfect Traeger Smoker Grill Recipes for you and those you love.

# Indexes in Alphabetical Order

**M**

**P**

**Q**

**R**

**S**

# Index of Ingredients

# R

# S

# T

CPSIA information can be obtained
at www.ICGtesting.com
Printed in the USA
BVHW090321040521
606332BV00006B/1393